Nepal as a Federal State

Lessons From Indian Experience

Nepal as a Federal State

Lessons From Indian Experience

Editor

V R Raghavan

Vij Books India Pvt Ltd
New Delhi (India)

Published by

Vij Books India Pvt Ltd

2/19, Ansari Road, Darya Ganj
New Delhi - 110002
Phones: 91-11-47340674, 91-11- 43596460
Fax: 91-11-47340674
e-mail : vijbooks@rediffmail.com
web : www.vijbooks.com

© **2013, Centre for Security Analysis, Chennai, India**

Centre for Security Analysis
"9-B" Ninth Floor,
Chesney Nilgiri, 71, Ethiraj Salai,
Egmore, Chennai-600008
Tamil Nadu, India
+91-44-65291889
office@csa-chennai.org
www.csa-chennai.org

First Published : 2013

Paperback Edition 2015

Contents

Acknowledgement

The Centre for Security Analysis (CSA) has undertaken a three year research project **Internal Conflicts and Transnational Consequences** supported by the John D and Catherine T MacArthur Foundation. This volume is part of the ongoing project and its publication has been possible by the project grant.

PROLOGUE

The Centre for Security Analysis (CSA) has been engaged in analysing internal conflicts in South and Southeast Asia with special emphasis on the consequences of such conflicts. This is a new approach to conflict management and subsequent resolution. Instead of focussing on the causes of the conflicts alone, CSA explored the consequences of the protracted conflicts – Northeast of India, Jammu and Kashmir, Naxalism, Myanmar, Nepal and Sri Lanka to examine the way consequences undermine the states' efforts to bring stability, development and peace to the region.

The CSA organised a study in 2010 to analyse the consequences of the conflict in Nepal. At that point of time, the Constitutional Assembly was engaged in framing the Constitution for Nepal which is yet to materialise. However, Nepal stands renamed "Federal Republic of Nepal" but is yet to acquire federal character due to lack of consensus over the model of federalism. Nepal's idea of federalism has not yet cristallised.

The central lesson from Nepal is that all parties involved need to have clear objectives and a strategy to manage the consequences of internal conflict. The Nepal Maoists went into a revolution without a post revolution strategy. After the Monarchy has been displaced, they were unable to form a government by themselves. Such consequences had not been visualized and planned in the Maoist strategy. Each consequence creates a new dynamic for the conflict and it is important to not only anticipate the consequences but also strategize its management. Both the objective and the consequence should be studied and understood carefully.

Nepal has a multi-ethnic, multi-linguistic and multi-cultural society with 101 caste/ethnic groups, 91 linguistic groups and nine religious groups. And this diversity is not represented in the structure of government at any level.

The Hill-Hindu high castes — Brahmins and Chhetris — who constitute only 31 per cent of the total population occupy the lion's share of key positions in the country's social, economic and political power structures. Following the Comprehensive Peace Agreement, there has been a distinct rise of ethnicity as a socio-political dynamic among the excluded groups. The rationale for federalism is to ensure that the new set up addresses the issues of inclusion, decentralisation, balanced and sustainable regional development and a sense of national unity. Instead, a strong preference for a future Nepal based on ethnic, geographic and political basis has emerged.

Political parties are divided over the scope and the process of restructuring the Nepali state. Two different models of restructuring were submitted by State Restructuring Commission. The majority has proposed to divide the country into 11 provinces with priority rights to dominant ethnic groups at the local level. The report prepared by the dissenting members has suggested forming of six provinces including two in the plains and four in hills and mountains on the basis of economic viability. United Communist Party of Nepal (Maoist) [(UCPN-(M)] and Madeshi Front advocate identity based restructuring whereas Nepali Congress and Communist Party of Nepal (Unified Marxist Leninist) [CPN (UM-L)] oppose this and are in favour of economically viable provinces as an alternative. While federalism is generally accepted as a guiding principle, the approach, type and other nuances are yet to be discussed and accepted. A politically significant minority of Nepali population opposes federalism altogether.

Those who favour federalism believe that it will result in decentralisation and thus greater access to decision making, exercise control over state services and ensure equitable representation. On the other hand those who oppose it express concern about unity of the country. Federalism is a dynamic process wherein the state has to develop and respond to the changing conditions over time. Two of the biggest challenges Nepal faces are to establish mutual trust between its key actors and public acceptance of the form of federalism. Nepal can draw immensely from success and innovations of Indian federation.

Against this backdrop, CSA in collaboration with Centre for South Asian Studies, Kathmandu organized a seminar *Nepal as a Federal; State: Lessons from Indian Experience* wherein different facets of federalism were explored by experts from India and Nepal. Indian Ambassador to Nepal Mr Jayant Prasad and Mr Rajendra Mahato, President Sadbhawana Party and Minister for Health and Population, Government of Nepal asserted that federalism was necessary for economic prosperity and proportional development. Mr G K Pillai former Union Home Secretary gave an insightful talk on Indian experiences of federalism.

This volume will be of much interest to policy planners, academia and all those concerned with the on going political processes in Nepal.

Introduction

This book is an outcome of a significant conference on "Federalism in Nepal: Lessons from Indian Experience" which was jointly organized by the Centre for South Asian Studies (CSAS), Kathmandu and the Chennai based Centre for Security Analysis (CSA) on August 30-31, 2012. One of the hallmarks was the participation of erudite paper presenters and prominent individuals from India who came to Kathmandu solely for this event; this in many ways, served as a cross-learning exercise designed to cater for a better understanding of the federal structure so successfully in operation in India for over 60 years.

The CSAS has over the past few years tried to bring in authorities on the subject to speak on various facets of a democratic and a forward looking constitution, on federalism, secularism and also on other issues of strategic importance for the benefit of intellectuals, policy makers and political leaders of Nepal. The CSA and CSAS are associated in several regional and international networks of think-tanks. It was under this aegis that the two institutions came together to hold the conference. The conference was attended by about 50 Nepali participants ranging from political party leaders to academics, economists and media persons. This book which has incorporated all the papers presented in the conference have dealt on the various working models of federalism, how to establish laws and build institutions on which social order, justice and democracy depend.

The whole essence of federalism is that each social, economic and political entity can pursue their individual dreams as individual states but still come together as one national family, to ensure that the future generations of the nation can also pursue their dreams and aspirations. Unity is not uniformity but diversity need not also mean division. Trouble starts when for political ends, cultural, religious and linguistic diversity is mis-used for dividing and destabilizing society and elections are reduced to becoming a contest of one-upmanship between various castes and ethnic groups. Many countries have progressed and prospered under the federal set-up - India, Germany, Switzerland are some cases in point. There are many examples also of societies breaking up and nations plummeting to civil war precisely for being unable to develop a healthy political culture and an all- acceptable structure during the formative years of constitution drafting and democracy building.

Unfortunately it was on the very issue of federalism that consensus could not be reached among major political parties that led to the demise of the first-ever Constituent Assembly in Nepal without completing its primary mandate. Instead of abandoning hope and embracing only blame, Nepal has wasted six more months in reaching a broad understanding in devising a workable political model. Foremost problem has been lack of direction from the top. In the case of India, Prime Minister Nehru's exemplary leadership, large-heartedness and visionary statesmanship provided 17 years of uninterrupted stability in the initial years of the Indian Republic. This proved crucial for the tenacity and durability of the Indian democracy. At the Constituent Assembly Pandit Nehru said, "Our first task is to free India through a new Constitution, to feed our starving people, to clothe the naked masses, to give every Indian the complete opportunity to develop himself according to his capacity. A constitution not able to solve the problem of the poor and the starving is merely a paper constitution - useless and purposeless."

His central concern for secularism, cultural pluralism, communal harmony and toleration made India what it is today - an emerging economic and military giant of the 21st century within a lifetime of a single generation. Of course, there are problems which still exist but they are constantly evolving and resolving within the broad parameters of the Indian constitution. There is a lot to learn from the achievement and the mistakes, the trials and tribulation in India for the Nepalese - to study and thereby lay a durable mechanism.

Unfortunately, political instability has been Nepal's foremost problem. Nepal did not have a single Prime Minister completing his full term in office ever since Prime Minister Juddha Shumsher abdicated in favor of his nephew in 1945 and left for self-exile in Dehra Dun. Even after the historic change of 2006, there have already been five Prime Ministers. This has impacted negatively on governance as government officials are also routinely transferred each time the government is replaced. While one hopes to overcome these challenges, the Nepalese people are getting impatient on issues of economic progress, political stability, delivery of basic services by the state and moreover a secure environment for them to live and work. How a federal structure carved out in a complex mosaic of Nepali society with 101 declared ethnic groups cater to this desire for good governance is another challenge that Nepal needs to chart out without further delay.

The Ambassador of India to Nepal Shri Jayant Prasad has always encouraged and contributed immensely to the understanding of the subject by his erudite opening remarks.

The Chief Guest at the Conference, Minister Rajendra Mahato stated in his speech that the political parties were working towards an amicable solution to the current deadlock in the country that would lead towards elections and thereby a new constitution. Minister Mahato, a seasoned politician from the Terai remarked that since federalism was there to stay, the only option was to devise a workable model of the federal structure instead of criticizing the very concept itself. His emphasis on federal structure for Nepal reflects a meaningful public discourse in Nepal.

Mr. G.K. Pillai with his long experience in working the Indian federal system made a significant contribution to the conference. His paper is incorporated in this volume. Readers will gain from his vast reservoir of understanding of the practice of federal set up in the various tiers of governance in India and its relevance to Nepal.

We would also like to thank the paper presenters, Prof. Lok Raj Baral, Mr. Madhu Raman Acharya, Dr. Shambhu Ram Simkhada, Ms. Menuka Guruswamy, Lalit Basnet and Raju Chapagain, Mr. Chiran Thapa and Ratna Sansar Shrestha for their analysis of the issues involved. Their papers which are published in this book are a learned and wide ranging compilation of ideas and concepts of immense value in taking forward the idea of Nepal as a Federal State. CSA had earlier commissioned a study of the economic consequences of the conflict in Nepal by Dr Hari Bansh Jha. His analytical paper is relevant at this juncture and has been included in this volume. We are also thankful to Dr. Shekhar Koirala, Dr. Geeta Madhavan and Prof. Sushil Raj Pandey for chairing the various sessions of the conference.

Brig. K. Srinivasan (Retd) of the CSA and Ramesh Timasina, Renisha Khadga and Daya Raj Subedi of the CSAS made an outstanding contribution in organizing this event.

Nishchal N Pandey   V R Raghavan
Director   President
Centre for South Asian Studies   Centre for Security Analysis
Kathmandu, Nepal   Chennai, India

Nepal as a Federal State: Lessons From the Indian Experience

Ambassador Jayant Prasad

Hon'ble Rajendra Mahato, President, Sadbhavana Party and Minister for Health & Population, Dr. Nishchal Pandey, Director, Centre for South Asian Studies (CSAS), Gen V.R. Raghavan, President, Centre for Security Analysis (CSA), and Mr. G.K. Pillai, former Home Secretary, Government of India, distinguished panellists and participants, ladies and gentlemen.

The Centre for South Asian Studies and the Centre for Security Analysis have to be complimented for organizing this conference on a critical and, arguably, divisive issue facing Nepal in finalizing its new Constitution. I do fervently hope that the exchanges here will shine some light on the path that lies ahead. For Nepal, the choices are more difficult than the one faced by India when India's Constituent Assembly began to consider the outline of our Constitution on 9th December 1946, just before our independence. In respect of federalism, India already had provinces in British India. For Nepal, which had no such previous familiarity, federalism implies a reinvention of its domestic political structures and system of governance. It is a more daunting task than the one we faced in India.

I am happy to offer brief remarks on the Indian experience of federalism to an informed audience of scholars and practitioners. I am here to share my thoughts on the subject not in the hope that they prove instructive for the current debates in Nepal, but to provide the context and background of India's democratic experiment, which includes federalism. The nature of federalism in Nepal will necessarily have to conform to the genius and needs of the Nepalese people.

India is a "Union of States" organized as a sovereign, secular, socialist, democratic republic. The words, "federal" and "federalism" do not feature in the text of the Constitution. The Union is unalterable and inviolable, but not so the States and their boundaries. India is not a federation created by an agreement among the States to join the Union. Nor do the constituent States have the right to secede from the Union. Even so, as the 1994 judgment of the nine-judge bench of the Supreme Court of India clearly established, federalism is a basic feature of India's constitution. India's States, according to the judgement (in the case, SR Bommai v Union of India, concerning the dismissal of BJP Governments in Madhya Pradesh, Himachal Pradesh and Rajasthan), "are neither satellites nor agents of the Centre" and "have as important a role to play in the political, social, educational and cultural life of the people as the Union."

Responding to the criticism that the draft Constitution had too much of centralization, and that States had been reduced to municipalities, in his speech in the Constituent Assembly on 25th November 1949, the penultimate day before the adoption of the Constitution, the Chairman of the Drafting Committee, B.R. Ambedkar, clarified the fundamental principle on which rests the relationship between the Centre and the States:

> "The basic principle of federalism is that the legislative
> and executive authority is partitioned between the Centre
> and the State not by any law to be made by the Centre but
> by the Constitution itself. This is what our Constitution
> does.... The Centre cannot, by its own will, alter the
> boundary of that partition. Nor can the judiciary."

The overriding powers of the Union in times of a grave emergency arising in the country can turn India into a unitary State. But the invocation of these powers is meant only for extreme contingencies. The Supreme Court's jurisdiction covering disputes between the Union and States has helped establish a healthy equilibrium between the Union and its constituent States.

Just as the inspiration of independent India's foreign policy lay in India's struggle for freedom, so it was with India's federalism. India's national leaders came from different parts of the country. Their self-image was made up of multiple identities. As they took their places centre stage as combatants for national independence, they also remained leaders of their respective communities. This, in turn, helped in maintaining a balance between the centre and the regions.

Federalism in India is not just a constitutional construct, a manner of organisation of its political structure by demarcating competencies between the Union and State Governments. It is a living and growing idea, whose progressive concretisation is intermediated by India's evolution. The pluralist impulse in India has become stronger over time, and is now better subsumed and articulated within constitutional boundaries.

The State Restructuring Commission, set up in 1954, began the process of remaking the Indian Union from 1956. We now have 28 States and 7 Union Territories. The States were variously constituted over time, on the basis of linguistic boundaries, tribal identities, and, as in the case of Uttarakhand, Jharkhand and Chattisgarh, regional and territorial backwardness.

The evolving nature of Indian federalism is not confined to the number of States. It includes the subtle changes in relations between the Union and State Governments and through the 73rd and 74th Constitution Amendment Acts of 1993, which further devolved authority and self-governance to entities at the sub-state level. Moreover, the discretionary element in the allocation of resources by the Union Government to the States has been reduced by the conventions developed on financial transfers under the Seventh Schedule of the Constitution, by the Finance Commission, and by the Union Ministries and Planning Commission for specified projects and programmes.

The unitary bias in India's Constitution comes from several sources. Given the trauma of partition and the challenge of integration of the princely states, including the outbreak of hostilities related to Jammu & Kashmir, maintenance of national integrity became an important priority for the members of our Constituent Assembly. The compulsion to create a centralised state was buttressed by the meltdown of administrative control and the inability to contain the communal violence that accompanied India's partition, as also the armed uprising in Telengana led by the Communist

Party of India. The progressive social and economic outlook of the Indian National Congress, reflected in the AICC Resolution on Objectives and Economic Programme in its first post-independent session in November 1947, also necessitated the centralized direction of Government.

A longer term factor that worked towards India's centralized federalism was the colonial subjugation of India by a singular power. It was natural that opposition to it would be expressed in terms of singularity of a united nation, and as part of the effort to forge unity cutting across regions, religions, caste, race, ethnicity, language and cultures. Nationalist historians extolled the virtues of India's historic unifiers and State builders, Ashoka and Akbar. There was an entrenched belief among people across India that the British prevailed and ruled over the country for so long because of India's predisposition to disunity and the absence of nationalistic spirit. Indeed, in this respect, Nepal was seen as a contrast to India. Jawaharlal Nehru wrote in the *Discovery of India*, with a sense of admiration, that Nepal was the only truly independent nation of South Asia. And, as the day of India's independence drew closer, the national leaders became convinced that India could not possibly attain its true potential without effective direction being provided by a strong central Government.

Two new factors have affected Indian federalism since the 1990s. The first is the politics of coalition that shapes the Union Government. The coalitions at the centre now comprise multiple regional parties, whose leaders straddle state and central politics. These smaller parties are critical to ensuring stability to the coalitions. Indeed, the national parties in India cannot hope to constitute a government without regional and local allies. Leaders of regional parties at the centre exercise power disproportionate to their strength in parliament. As a consequence, in actual practice, the States of the Indian Union exercise a greater measure of autonomy than is allowed to them strictly on the basis of the division of legislative and executive powers provided in the Constitution.

Another significant change has come about as a consequence of the unshackling of the Indian economy, the deregulation of domestic business, the de-licensing of industry, and encouragement to investments. This has led to competition and differentiation among States which are increasingly asserting their autonomy in shaping their growth and development.

The Indian Constitution may not be a perfect text. It has, however, a distinct merit, that of its adjustable capacity, especially in amendment of its provisions, to grow in accord with the contingencies of India's evolution and the aspirations of its citizens. By ensuring that a problem in one or many States of the Union does not consume the country as a whole, the federal structure has helped maintain India's unity and integrity. It has been a way of holding together a heterogeneous country.

Indeed, India's relative stability and progress would not have been possible without the institutions to promote democracy and federalism. As an intrinsic element of India's democracy, federalism has contributed to respect for plurality and inclusive governance. That, in a nutshell, is the broad lesson from the Indian experience.

Federalism: The Indian Experience

Gopal K Pillai

The word "Federalism" or "Federal" does not appear in the Indian constitution even once. This has led many scholars to question whether India is at all a federal state. The general consensus is that India is a quasi-federal state and is slowly moving towards what is being popularly written about as "cooperative federalism". The Indian constitution, in many respects is a unique document. It can only be understood, in the historical context in which it was drafted-namely the Government of India Act 1935, the partition of India, the accession and integration of the princely states and the overwhelming concern of the Constituent Assembly for the unity and integrity of post partition India. It therefore took shape as a Union of States with a strong Centre, rather than as a loose federation of states that was being discussed at the initial drafting stage.

As the Justice Punchhi Commission put it succinctly, "The Constituent Assembly, through several expert committees, devised the notion of 'Domain Specification' for distribution of powers. Hierarchical, non-hierarchical and non-centralized distribution of powers was embedded within the federal framework. The aim was to provide the Union an organic linkage with the units to ensure unity of purpose and commonality of interests. The underlying and uncompromising assumption was that the proposed Union had to be indestructible. Dr. B.R. Ambedkar, Chairman of the Drafting Committee of the Constitution of India, made use of the term 'Union' clear when he stated in the Constituent Assembly that "the use of the term 'Union' is deliberate...I can tell you why the Drafting Committee used it. The Drafting Committee wanted to make it clear that though India was to be a federation, the federation was not the result of an agreement by the states to join a federation and that the federation not being the result of an agreement, no state has the right to secede from it. 'It also explains the fact that the Union is indestructible but not the states; their identity can be altered or even obliterated. Explaining the purpose, Dr. Ambedkar emphasised: the Draft Constitution has sought to forge means and methods whereby India will have be federation and at the same time will have uniformity in all basic matters which are essential to maintain the unity of the country."

It would be useful to recapitulate the essential features of the Indian Constitution, so as to understand why most scholars refer to it as quasi-federal rather than a purely federal set up. The Union List contains 97 items of which the more important are defence, foreign affairs, banking, currency, coinage, union taxes and duties, telecommunication. The Constitution gives Parliament exclusive powers with respect to foreign affairs, including all matters which bring the Union into relation with any foreign country. Furthermore, treaty making and implementation of Treaties is a subject of Union Legislation. Article 253 ensures legislative competence to Parliament to pass laws with respect to matters in the State Lists, in so far as it is necessary to implement any Treaty, Agreement or Convention with a foreign country or any decision made at any International Conference, Association or other body. Entry 31 places every aspect of communication with the Union Government. This includes posts and telegraphs, telephones, wireless, broadcasting and other like forms of communication.

The list of exclusive State powers has sixty six entries. The important entries include public order, police, state civil service, public health and sanitation, local communication, agriculture, fisheries, land and land revenue, education. The Constitution of India also provides for areas of concurrent jurisdiction with equal competence for the Union Government and the State Government, although the central law would prevail over the state law unless it had special features which were concurred in by the Union Government, after the passage of the Union Legislation. The Constitution also gave exclusive jurisdiction to the Supreme Court to decide upon disputes between the Union and the states or between the states.

Taking note of the diverse ethnic reality and the need to protect the culture, customs, land rights and ethnic identity of the various tribal groups, a specific sub-text of the Constitution namely the Fifth and Sixth Schedules to the Constitution have been provided. This is a unique feature in the Indian Constitution. They provide a new dimension to the concept of Federalism as this provision is intended for tribal groups within states and provide additional protection to vulnerable tribal groups who reside in specific areas within a state. The land rights and the customs, culture of these vulnerable groups are given constitutional protection and excluded from any attempt even by the state to change these provisions. Such measures are necessary to give confidence to these vulnerable groups that even though they may be part of a larger state, specific protection is given and they need not fear, even if a minority that the State can trample over their rights, especially over land which is vital to their very survival. Looking back after 60 years, one can say that the provisions of the Sixth Schedule, which is applicable in the North-Eastern states have by and large served their original purpose and protected these communities. On the other hand, in the Fifth Schedule areas, one notes that land alienation had taken place to a significant extent, despite express provisions to the contrary and these communities have not been fully able to take advantage of the specific protections available. This, regardless of specific provisions that the Governor of the state has responsibility (independent of the state government) for overseeing the implementation of the Fifth Schedule, which unfortunately was not exercised.

The most important aspect of federalism is of course, the aspect of financial resources which are essential to carry out the responsibilities enumerated in the Constitution for both the Union and the states. Here the Constitution has, apart from giving certain exclusive powers of taxation to the Union and the states also established a unique system to transfer resources from the Union to the states in the following forms:-

(1) Through the levy by the Centre, but assignment in whole of the proceeds of certain taxes (Art 269)

(2) Through mandatory sharing of the proceeds of Income Tax (Art 270)

(3) Through permissive participation in the proceeds of the Union Excise Duties (Art 272)

(4) Through Statutory Grants-in-Aid of the revenues of the states (Art 275)

(5) Through grants for any Public purpose (Art 282)

Subsequently Art 272 was deleted and the Constitution (80th Amendment Act 2000) provided for sharing of all net proceeds of Union Taxes and Duties with the states.

The provision in the Indian Constitution for the setting up of a Finance Commission every five years is a unique concept. It has strengthened fiscal federalism in India. The Union Government having regularly followed this provision and accepting the recommendations of the Finance Commission has ensured that framework of Centre-State financial relations embodied in the Constitution stands the test of time and works fairly and smoothly.

With this extremely brief overview of the salient features of the Indian Constitution, let us look at how the system has actually worked on the ground during the last sixty two years. Broadly, these could be grouped into four phases:

1950-67: Domination of the Congress Party at the Centre and the states

1967-77: Rise of Regional Parties; Emergency; and further erosion of the Congress party

1977-1991: Era of coalition governments

1991-2012: Economic liberalization; globalization and its impact: rise of regional parties and coalition governments.

During the period 1950-63, India was ruled by the Indian National Congress both at the Centre and at the State level. The towering personality of Pt Jawaharlal Nehru was key factor as the nascent Indian State struggled to establish parliamentary democracy, the rule of law and social justice. Pt Nehru was a great democrat and a consensus builder. His thousands of letters to Chief Ministers of various states on the problems facing the nation and how they were to be tackled and inviting their suggestions and opinions paved the foundations for federalism to be established in India. It was not that there were no problems during this period. There were major problems like the accession and integration of States, the formation of linguistic states, the anti-Hindi agitation, and abolishment of the Zamindari System, the Center's move to empower itself with powers for land Acquisition-a subject reserved for the states, insurgency in the North-eastern states and the creation of new states from out of the states of Assam, the Punjab problem. Each one of these tested the constitutional framework and found it flexible enough to meet the aspirations of the multi-lingual, multi-ethnic, multi-religious mosaic that was India, as forged by the founding fathers of the Indian Constitution. A great advantage, it was to have the same Government at the Centre and the states and the presence of Jawaharlal Nehru as the Prime Minister of India. Any one of these issues could have snowballed into a major row affecting the federal nature of the country, but timely and sometimes delayed responses in a spirit of understanding and compromise assuaged the feelings of the state or the region or the community and helped to strengthen the federal relationship. It is not as if during this period mistakes and arbitrary actions were absent. The dismissal of the first Communist State, Government in Kerala elected by popular vote will remain a black spot on Indian Democracy. So also decisions were made which created further problems which last to this day. The treatment and classification of the State of Manipur, which had a Constitution and legislature as a Class C State had repercussions which reverberate to this day. So was the case with the creation of the State of Nagaland in 1963. There was a growing realization that the problems of this huge sub-continent could not be solved from Delhi. The country was too vast and diverse for a Central Government to be able to tackle all the issues. The rise of regional parties which reflected this ethos could not be stopped and with the 1967 elections which reflected this fractured mandate, the time had come to seriously introspect on Centre-State relations. However, the 1971 war and the landslide victory of Mrs Indira Gandhi and subsequently, the imposition of Emergency during 1975-77, actually resulted in over-centralisation and was a setback to a healthy federal set-up. Two issues, namely the imposition of Presidents rule by dismissing State Governments and the role of the Governor came into sharp focus during this period. Two important reports namely the Rajamannar Committee Report (set up by the Tamil Nadu Government) and the Memorandum on Centre-State relations published by the West Bengal Government-both calling for increased autonomy to the state governments reflected this growing disenchantment with an apparently too powerful Central Government. The 1980's saw increasing confrontation between the Central Government and the state governments run by regional parties. In the light of this background and ambience, Mrs Indira Gandhi, announced in Parliament on March 24, 1983, the proposal to appoint a Commission on Centre-State relations.

The Sarkaria Commission Report, although not accepted *in toto,* gave an opportunity to the states to reflect and articulate their concerns on the federal set up. Many of the concerns of the state, especially in respect of the use of Article 356, role of Governors and decentralization were reflected in the Final Report. The conventions and guidelines prescribed in the report were imbibed by the Central Government and with new Supreme Court guidelines on judicial review of Central Government action has resulted in restoring the balance of power in this regard. The important recommendations accepted, include the role of Governors, constitution of Inter State Council, Decentralization, including the establishment of local self governing bodies finally bore fruition with the 73rd and 74th Constitutional Amendment Acts, which conferred constitutional status on Panchayati Raj Institutions, as well as Municipalities. The other major recommendation accepted by the Government was that the proceeds of Corporate Tax may be shareable with the states.

Significant developments thereafter were the growing economic liberalization, globalization of the world economy, the establishment of the WTO, increasing concern over climate change, all of which seriously affected the state governments who felt that they had limited say on matters which affected not only the people of their state but the subject matter which was exclusively allotted to the states under the Indian Constitution. Agriculture was a key irritant. State had exclusive rights over agriculture which was a state subject. But the Central Government was negotiating agricultural issues like tariffs and access, which seriously affected the livelihoods of millions of subsistence farmers living in the states. The Central Government did consult the state governments and elements of the stakeholders, but in view of the complexity of the subject and developing country coalitions at negotiating fora, not all the concerns could be accommodated. Hence, the growing demand that the constitution be amended to allow Parliament to approve/ratify international agreements, as is being done by some countries.

Although, the 73rd and 74th Constitutional Amendments have given constitutional protection to local self governing bodies, the devolution of administrative and financial powers has been niggardly and the main culprits are the state governments who fear loss of power and influence to the Panchayati Raj Institutions and Municipalities. The process of devolution has begun and it is only a matter of time before these Institutions become self governing in reality also. The reservation of seats for women in these local bodies from 33.3% to 50% is resulting in new forms of empowerment and in a generation or so, will change the face of rural leadership in the country.

Taking the above factors into consideration, the UPA Government on April 27, 2007, set up the second Commission on Centre-State relations Chaired by the retired Supreme Court Chief Justice, M.M. Punchhi.

One significant term of reference to the Commission was to make recommendations on the role, responsibility, and jurisdiction of the Centre vis-a vis states during major and prolonged outbreaks of communal violence, caste violence or any other social conflict leading to prolonged and escalated violence. A related term of reference was on the need to set up a Central Law Enforcement Agency empowered to take up *suo-moto* investigation of crimes having inter-state ramifications with serious implications on national security and/or international ramifications.

Other terms apart from review of the Centre-State relations included need for unified and integrated domestic market, economic and financial relations, mechanism for inter-governmental consultations, local governments and decentralized governance, long gestation mega projects involving more than one state, etc.

The potential areas of conflict are in the legislative, administrative, judicial and financial sectors.

In the legislative field, the areas of conflict have been few and where these have occurred, have been resolved mainly through discussion or through reference to courts. The Constitution, here has formed the basis for judicial interpretation and there is a broad consensus to accept the rulings of the courts in this regard. The high respect, in which the higher courts are held especially the High Courts and the Supreme Court has facilitated easy acceptance of the court verdicts. But as the recent controversy over the establishment of the National Counter Terrorism Council (NCTC) has revealed, the states are very wary of any further encroachment into the states' jurisdiction and painstaking discussion and consultation is necessary to evolve a broad consensus among the states so that issues of national security do not get politicized or misunderstood as the Centre trying to erode further the state's powers. Mining and environment legislations are a potential source of conflict in the coming years.

In the administrative field, the All India Services were expected to provide the necessary coordination and ease potential areas of conflict. Arbitrary actions by some state governments against All India Service officers have led to friction in recent years. The action by the Central Government in not upholding the suspension of certain officers by the state government in recent times and the posting of an IPS officer who was being victimized by the stategovernment, to a Central Government post even in the absence of vigilance clearance by the state government are pointers to greater conflicts in this area in the future. Monitoring of police reforms is another area of friction as state governments consider it their exclusive domain, although the fallout could have larger implications for national security.

The Inter-State Council showed great promise, but in recent years, the meetings have been few and far and the Centre has not shown the keenness to have regular meetings and bring important issues for in-depth discussion with a view to find ways to resolve them.

It is the responsibility of the Central Government to take the initiative and move for greater consultation with the states. My own experience is that the state governments will be more than willing to go the extra mile to find a consensus, if they feel that the Central Government is willing to take their interests also into account. The meetings of the Zonal Council are a testimony to what can be achieved if regular meetings are held and channels of communication kept open. This enables regular exchange of views, avoids misunderstanding and ensures that situation do not go out of hand.

A more urgent issue is the large number of inter-state disputes, whether it is on boundary issues, migration or even on sharing of water. These require states to show a pragmatic vision and avoid jingoist posturing. Media and vested interests are a real threat to finding win-win solutions for such disputes. The Central Government in such cases has to play the role of honest broker and facilitate the states to find a win-win solution. This becomes a problem when coalition governments have partners from only one of the states and neutrality becomes suspect.

A major issue that will come into greater focus will be the interpretation of Article 355 of the Indian Constitution on the extent to which the Central Government can intervene in a state, even without the consent of the state, by sending in Armed Forces of the Union, if it feels that the internal disturbance is of such a magnitude that Central intervention is required to bring the disturbance under control. The Punchhi Commission has opined that Article 355 is substantive in nature and not just an advisory provision. The ramifications of this are currently being examined by the Central government, in consultation with the states. The Communal Violence Bill currently under consideration will test the political and federal basis of the Indian Constitution.

The introduction of a Uniform Value Added Tax (VAT) throughout the country was a signal success for fiscal federalism. The innovative suggestion to make one of the State Finance Ministers as the Chairman of the Committee considering the proposal and extensive consultations, helped in the easy passage of the proposal. The establishment of the Planning Commission through an executive order by the Centre, and the transfer of plan resources to the states through this mechanism, was initially objected to by the states as bypassing the constitutional framework of the Finance Commissions and giving another lever to the Central Government to control state finances. But, over the years, this objection has considerably muted and many states see this as another means of transfer of Central resources to the states. The Finance Commissions have also taken note of this mechanism, while formulating their recommendations.

The states, under the Indian Constitution have been exclusively earmarked substantive powers, and with substantial transfer of financial resources, are doing quite well. This is reflected in the fact that any politician would prefer to be the Chief Minister of State, rather than a Union Cabinet Minister.

Whether you call India a quasi-federal state or co-operative federalism, the most important point to be understood, is that it is always a work in progress. There is no strong centre – weak state or weak centre – strong state. Both the Centre and the states have to be strong, if a federal set up is to succeed. Both have their roles to play and accommodating genuine concerns of both the Centre and the state are essential if we want the country to progress. This requires constant interaction, not just when there is a problem to be resolved, but genuine dialogue and articulation of concerns on a regular basis. In South Asia, personal relations are more important and the politicians and bureaucrats who maintain good personal relations with their counterparts always find the going easier.

In a sense, many of the low hanging fruits in the quasi- federal set up have been harvested. Difficult issues in Centre- State relations and between states and between states and local bodies are looming and it will require wisdom and political leadership to smoothly navigate over the coming decades. I have no doubt that the Indian State will find its own solutions in the coming years.

Indian Federalism-That Which was not Constitutionally in Tender

Menaka Guruswamy

Introduction

Perhaps the most contested area when writing a constitution is federalism. Since no other arena of constitution-design has more implications on the nature of the character of a nation. By character I mean- the basis of identity of various communities within a new nation, fiscal or revenue sharing arrangements between units, and even the ability or inability of a unit to secede from that union. The quest for a state 'recognised' identity becomes a rallying point for movements within a new state, and hence a source of friction and breakdown of the constitution-making processes. A dialogue to enable consensus around the basis for recognition of a unit, is a critical element of successful constitution-making. And the absence of any such consensus is as Nepal has realised, debilitating for a constitution-making project.

Nepal's constitution-making project was intertwined with the peace process- integration of combatants and formation of government. The absence of a simple majority in the constituent assembly for any single political party rendered the absence of dialogue and consensus even more poisonous for constitution-making. Therefore, the constitution could not be crafted on the basis of a shared idea of a nation, or even less elegantly on the basis of numerical strength in the assembly.

In Nepal, federalism became a sticky issue within and outside the assembly. I shall discuss India's own experience of federalism in the context of constitution-making in the late 1940s and the federal dynamic as it played out post-independence, well into contemporary India. Perhaps specific political moments, constitutional choices and socio-political movements which have all impacted federalism in India, may be useful for Nepal's future conversations around federalism and constitution-making.

In this brief paper I shall discuss India's rather unique model of federalism. What makes the model itself rather unique is how the constitution-drafters envisaged a more unitary and less federal country in the text of the constitution. Yet, in contemporary India owing to a confluence of various factors like a resurgent Supreme Court, the growth of regional political parties in tandem with the emergence of coalition governments at the centre and the ability to amend the constitution – the country has become far more federal than was envisaged by the framers of the constitution. While the dynamic evolution of the country's polity and with it the constitution may well be indicative of the changes being experienced by a young nation- it also raises important questions in the context of the constitution design envisaged.

Is the federalism bought on by the Supreme Court, amendments made by Parliament to the Constitution, and the growth of regional political parties and the decline of Indian National Congress in tune with the almost unitary form of governance envisaged by the constitution drafters? Are the changed centre-state relations that we in contemporary India have become so familiar with - what the drafters intended? We shall examine the intention of the drafters as epitomised by Dr. Ambedkar, (the Chairman of the Drafting Committee of the Constitution) in his explanations to the Constituent Assembly of the federalism that he and his colleagues envisaged for the new nation.

Federalism

Conception of federalism:

Before we proceed to the federal model envisaged by the drafters of the Indian Constitution, let us examine a general conception of federalism. South African scholar Bertus De Villiers explains that "the Latin origin of federalism *foedus* signifies a covenant according to which the relationship between the national and regional units is characterised by partnership, trust, pursuance of common objectives, sharing and cooperation between spheres of government."[1] He adds that "partnership implies ultimate trust, joint objectives, and respect for separate identities."[2] Villiers is no doubt influenced by South Africa's challenges as a diverse nation with its many competing demands of recognition of various identities as well challenges sharing of resources- financial and otherwise.

A Federal Entity Distinguished from a Non-Federal one

De Villiers distinguishes a federal from a non-federal nation. And while doing so he manages to explain the essence of federalism. He writes that "the key aspect that makes federal systems unique from other forms of decentralised arrangements is that within federations the existence of multi- tiered governments and their powers are defined and protected in a written, entrenched constitution (for example, the United States of America, Germany, South Africa, Belgium and Australia)." De Villiers contrasts this with what he calls 'non-federal dispensations'. According to him this latter group of nations usually provide for regional autonomy in an act of parliament and therefore it is possible for parliament to expand, amend, override or revoke regional autonomy by a simple majority. De Villiers cites the United Kingdom, Italy, France, Namibia as examples of non-federal dispensations.[3]

De Villiers most interesting point is how he conceptualises the differences between federal and non-federal entities and their treatment of diversity. He writes that "in non-federal dispensations diversity is often viewed with suspicion and as a possible threat to national unity, while in federal dispensations the very nature of the organisation of authority and decision-making allows for diversity not only to exist but even to flourish."[4] He gives examples of states that have used federal principles to manage diversity while at the same time promote national unity –

---

[1] Bertus de Villiers, "Comparative Studies of Federalism: Opportunities and Limitations as applied to the protection of cultural groups" J. S. Afr. L. 2004, p 210

[2] ibid.

[3] Bertus de Villiers, "Comparative Studies of Federalism: Opportunities and Limitations as applied to the protection of cultural groups" J. S. Afr. L.. 2004, p 210.

[4] Ibid

by looking to Switzerland, Canada, India, Nigeria, Malaysia, Brazil and, more recently, Belgium, South Africa, Mexico and Russia."[5]

Finally, he arrives at a check list of what a federation would have in place:

- A written, entrenched constitution

- Each sphere of government is served by elected, responsible and accountable institutions on the basis of democratic principles;

- An independent judiciary;

- Representation is provided for regions within the national parliament; and

- Formal and informal arrangements are made for institutions, policies and processes that facilitate intergovernmental cooperation between the spheres of government."[6]

Relying on this theoretical treatment by De Villiers of federalism as a foundation we shall appreciate the choices made by India both at the time of its constitution-making process and post the adoption of the constitution. India with its model of federalism that is unique to it satisfies the De Villiers check list. First, the constitution itself is a written document that is well entrenched. Second, every sphere of government is elected. Third, it has an independent judiciary. Fourth, representation is provided for regions- or rather states organised along linguistic lines and finally there are arrangements that facilitate cooperation between different spheres of government. Now let us continue this conversation about India's rather unique model of federalism by looking to the constitution-crafting process and dealing with an exposition of federalism by Dr. B.R. Ambedkar- the Chairman of the drafting committee of the constitution.[7]

---

[5] Ibid

[6] Bertus de Villiers, "Comparative Studies of Federalism: Opportunities and Limitations as applied to the protection of cultural groups" 2004 J. S. Afr. L. 209-234

[7] The Drafting Committee was appointed on 29th August 1947 With Dr.Ambedkar as the Chairman. There were six other members and an advisor. The members were KanaiyalalManeklalMunshi, AlladiKrishnaswamyIyer, N GopalaswamiAyengar , B L Mitter, Mohammad Saadullah and D P Khaitan . The constitutional advisor was Sir BenegalNarsing Rau.

Indian federalism: At the time of constitution-making

The Draft Constitution and its Conception of the Dual Polity

Dr. B R Ambedkar while introducing the draft Constitution of India to the Constituent Assembly on November 4th, 1948 dealt with India's unique conception of federalism. He says;

> "The Draft Constitution is, a Federal Constitution in as much as it establishes what may be called a Dual Polity. This Dual Polity under the proposed Constitution will consist of the Union at the centre and the states at the local level. The points of difference between the American Federation and the Indian Federation are mainly two. In the USA this dual polity is followed by dual citizenship. In the USA there is a citizenship of the State....The proposed Indian constitution is a dual polity with a single citizenship. There is only one citizenship for the whole of India."[8]

He added that "The dual polity of the proposed Indian Constitution differs from the dual polity of the USA in another respect. In the USA the Constitutions of the Federal and the States Governments are loosely connected."[9]

Dr. Ambedkar distinguishes India's federalism from that of the United States in two major ways. One, that in India a person was a citizen of India only and not also of the state in which he/she resided. Second, that there is only one constitution that of the Republic of India whereas in the United States each state had a constitution, and in addition there was a federal constitution.

India – A Union of States

Dr. Ambedkar makes it clear that the Indian federation was actually a union of states with no right of secession by any state within it. He refers to the

---

[8] Dr. B R Ambedkar, Constituent Assembly Debates, Vol. VII (November 4th, 1948)
[9] Ibid.

draft text of the constitution- specifically Article 1(1) states that "India, that is Bharat, shall be a Union of States." This draft text was retained in the final version of the constitution, and Dr. Ambedkar's explanation of it provides great insight into the kind of federalism that was envisaged for India by its constitution-writers.

Dr. Ambedkar states, "Some critics have taken objection to the description of India in Article 1 of the Draft Constitution as a Union of States. It is said that the correct phraseology should be Federation of States. But I can tell you why the Drafting Committee has used it (the word Union). The Drafting Committee wanted to make it clear that though India was to be a federation, the federation was not the result of an agreement by the States to join in a Federation and that the federation not being the result of an agreement no State has the right to secede from it. The Federation is a Union because it is indestructible..........The Americans had to wage a civil war to establish that the States have no right of secession and that their Federation was indestructible. The Drafting Committee thought that it was better to make it clear at the outset than to leave it to speculation or to dispute."[10]

Dr. Ambedkar here distinguishes the origins of the United States- a country conceived of as a commonwealth of states. He tried to explain that in the case of the United States the states came together to form a union and a civil war was waged that eventually cemented that union. However, India commenced by being a union first as opposed to any sort of commonwealth of states. The states within the Indian union since they did not become a part of it by choice had no right to secede. In fact the historical and political context to this may well explain why the country was conceived of as a union first, and a loose federation after. The long and arduous negotiations with the many hundreds of princely states to join the union and in the case of a few notables one like Hyderabad- needing the threat of armed action to compel them might well explain this choice.

---

[10] Dr. BR Ambedkar, Constituent Assembly Debates, Vol. VII, November 4th, 1948

The Political Realities that Necessitated the Union of States

The historian Manu Bhagwanan for instance explains the times as they were.[11] He notes that the princely states first tried to stay out of the constituent assembly as they wanted to retain their own kingdoms. Upon being persuaded to join the assembly, they somewhat reluctantly agreed to join the new Union after signing agreements. The princely states signed these agreements after being cajoled by then Viceroy Lord Mountbatten, Jawaharlal Nehru and Sardar Patel. As Bhagwanan points out, the princely states agreed to accede to the union only with regard to foreign affairs, defence and communication.[12]Therefore, he observed that after independence the government of India led by Sardar Patel and V.P. Menon "worked tirelessly to eliminate old princely boundaries, merging princely territories with surrounding ones…..to transfer all powers to the central government."[13]

This was the context that led Dr.Ambedkar and his colleagues to craft what was essentially a federation in name, but a union in character which the states had not come together to form, but were merged into. Therefore, boundaries were not fixed at the time of independence but the new constitution allowed the parliament to redraw boundaries and rename states.[14]And the Congress-dominated Parliament did exactly that they redrew the boundaries of the princely states, merging them with other states and changed names. All that could be done to solidify the Union, and create a new Indian identity. This shall be discussed in more detail in the next section.

Division of Powers between the Union and the States in the Indian Constitution

The Constitution that was finally adopted provided for a unique form of federalism that was more unitary and less conventionally federal. For instance, Article 3 provides that parliament may by law form new states,

---

[11] Manu Bhagavan, Princely states and the making of Modern India: Internationalism, constitutionalism and the post colonial moment, 46 (3) *The Indian Economic and Social History Review,* 427-456(2009).

[12] Bhagavan at 431

[13] Bhagavan at 431

[14] Articles 1 and 3 of the Constitution of India, 1950.

alter the areas, boundaries and names of existing states. Clearly, a state had no specific right to exist in a certain form if Parliament thought otherwise. And, the corollary of this is that given that the number and form of states is not fixed and therefore not finite, there are new demands in contemporary India for the formation of new states. An example of this is the agitation for the state of Telangana to be carved out of the existing state of Andhra Pradesh.

Yet, there was some effort to provide for some legislative power to the states as well. Therefore, Article 245 states that Parliament may make laws for the whole or any part of the territory of India, and the Legislature of a State may make laws for the whole or any part of the State. Legislative power was divided into three lists one each for the Union, and the states and a third one called the concurrent list – areas in which either could make laws.[15] Yet if there was an area not enumerated in the concurrent or state list then parliament would have the 'exclusive power to make law' with respect to that matter.[16] If there was any inconsistency between the laws of the union and the state then parliament triumphed.[17] And finally the Constitution makes it clear as to what shall be the source of major power within the country – the Union. Therefore, it provides that the executive power of every State shall be so exercised as not to impede or prejudice the exercise of the executive power of the Union, and the executive power of the Union shall extend to the giving of such directions to a State as may appear to the Government of India to be necessary for that purpose.[18]Therefore, the larger meta-structure of the division of powers between the centre and the states- allowed for three lists of legislative powers. One for the Union, second for the states and the last a concurrent list. These shall be discussed in further detail.

---

[15] Article 246. Provides that Subject-matter of laws made by Parliament and by the Legislatures of States.—- Union List, State List Concurrent List (idea from Australia)- all in the Seventh Schedule. " exclusive power to make laws"

[16] 248. Residuary powers of legislation.— lie with Parliament. (1) Parliament has exclusive power to make any law with respect to any matter not enumerated in the Concurrent List or State List.

(2) Such power shall include the power of making any law imposing a tax not mentioned in either of those Lists.

[17] 251. Inconsistency between laws made by Parliament under articles 249 and 250 and laws made by the Legislatures of States then parliament triumphs.

[18] Article 257, Constitution of India

Flexibility in federalism - What Enables Federalism to Evolve?

Flexibility in the federal structure - Ambedkar in the Constituent Assembly

The drafters of the constitution envisaged India to be flexible in that it would be federal or unitary depending on the context and the challenges facing the country. As Ambedkar explained:

> "All federal systems including the American are placed in a tight mould of federalism. No matter what the circumstances, it cannot change its form and shape. It can never be unitary. On the other hand the Draft Constitution can be both unitary as well as federal according to the requirements of time and circumstances. In normal times, it is framed to work as federal system. But in times of war it is so designed as to make it work as though it was a unitary system. Once the President issues a proclamation which he is authorised to do under the provisions of Article 275 the whole scene can become transformed and the State becomes a unitary state."[19]

Dr. Ambedkar was referring to what is now Article 352 of the Constitution that provides for the proclamation of emergency. For such a proclamation the President must be satisfied that a grave emergency exists whereby the security of India is threatened, by war or external aggression or armed rebellion. The President may, by Proclamation, make a declaration to that effect in respect of the whole or part of the country.

Weaknesses of rigidity and legalism: how have these been addressed by the drafters in India

Dr. Ambedkar worried about what he considered were the two weaknesses of Federalism – rigidity and legalism. In his own words as he addressed the Constituent Assembly;

---

[19] Dr. BR Ambedkar, Constituent Assembly Debates, Vol. VII (November 4th, 1948)

"There are two weaknesses from which Federation is alleged to suffer. One is rigidity and the other is legalism. That these are faults inherent in Federalism, there can be no dispute. A Federal Constitution cannot but be a written Constitution and a written Constitution must necessarily be a rigid Constitution. A Federal Constitution means division of Sovereignty by no less a sanction than that of the law of the Constitution between the Federal Government and the States, with two necessary consequences (1) that any invasion by the Federal Government in the field assigned to the States and vice versa is a breach of the Constitution, and (2) such breach is a justiciable matter to be determined by the Judiciary only."[20]

Dr. Ambedkar and the Constituent Assembly's solution to these twin problems were to ensure that Parliament would have overwhelming superiority over the State legislatures. Therefore, Article 249 grants Parliament the power to legislate with respect to a matter in the State List in the national interest. Article 250 enables Parliament to legislate in any matter in the State list if a proclamation of emergency is in operation. And, Article 252 enables Parliament to legislate for two or more States by consent and adoption of such legislation by any other State. And the other major method adopted to enable flexibility as explained by Dr.Ambedkar was "the second means adopted to avoid rigidity and legalism is the provision for facility with which the Constitution could be amended. [21]

Finally, Dr.Ambedkar spoke of another way in which the drafters created a unique way to ensure that while the country would have a federation, while also having an abiding uniformity in essential mechanisms of governance. Therefore, Dr.Ambedkar says that "the Draft Constitution has sought to forge means and methods whereby India will have Federation and at the same time will have uniformity in all basic matters which are essential to maintain unity of the country. The means adopted by the draft

---

[20] Dr. BR Ambedkar, Constituent Assembly Debates, Vol. VII (November 4th, 1948)
[21] Ibid.

Constitution were three:(1) A single judiciary, (2) Uniformity in fundamental laws - civil and criminal, and (3) a common all-Indian civil service to man important posts."[22]

Fiscal Federalism and the Powerful Union

The Constitution also maintains the domination of the Union over the States in fiscal matters, cementing the case that India is in terms of the text of the constitution more unitary and less federal in nature. Arshi Khan writes that the Constitution via Articles 286 and 276 (2) puts restrictions on the taxation powers of the states.[23] Khan points out that the Constitution distinguishes between the legislative power to levy a tax and the power to appropriate the proceeds of a tax so levied. By this Khan means that the legislative power pertaining to taxation is divided between Union and state governments by means of specific 'entries' in the Union list (82-92B) and the state list (45-63). According to Khan, the major objectives of federal fiscal transfer are 'to eliminate vertical and horizontal imbalances'.

Yet, Khan clarifies that all taxes and duties levied by the Union are not meant entirely for its own purposes. For instance, Khan writes that revenues from certain taxes and duties levied by it are totally assigned to or shared with states. But adds that customs duties, corporation tax, taxes on the capital value of assets (entries 83, 85 and 86 of the Union list) and fees in respect of matters in the Union list are levied, collected and wholly appropriated by the Union. Finally, Khan notes that borrowing powers (Articles 292 and 293) rest mostly with the Union."[24]

It is not that the states cannot levy taxes. They can and such areas of legislative power to levy tax include for instance Items 45-63 of List II of Schedule VII of the Constitution. These include the ability to tax in the area of land revenue, agricultural income, taxes on lands and buildings, taxes on mineral rights (subject to Union laws on mineral development), taxes on electricity and on entry of goods into a local area for consumption or sale amongst many others.

---

[22] Dr. BR Ambedkar, Constituent Assembly Debates, Vol. VII, November 4th, 1948

[23] Arshi Khan, "Situating Federalism, Minorities and Communalism in India's Polity," 4 *European Yearbook of Minority Issues* (2004-5) 85.

[24] Ibid.

The Evolution of Federalism in Contemporary India

Given this brief discussion of the Constitutional text that apparently locates much power with the Union and far less with the states, the subsequent development of India as a far more federal nation is a matter of some intrigue.This growth of India into a federal nation is conceivably at odds with the intended constitutional design and the text that was initially adopted. There are four features that M.P. Singh identifies that have contributed to the growth of federalism in the country.

These factors include the ability of new states to be created, since the constitution never put a limit on the crafting of new states. And therefore there are presently twenty-eight states and seven union territories that comprise India today. As M.P. Singh writes, the rise of fragmented ethnic identities and strong micro-regionalism has forced the short-sighted union government to create new states, often disregarding administrative rationality and financial viability."[25]

Constitutional amendments in the form of the Seventy-Third and Seventy-Fourth Constitutional Amendments in 1992 heralded what Singh calls "a new phase of revival and reorganisation in local self-government in rural and urban India".[26] The *panchayats* were brought back as the third tier of governance by these amendments.

The third factor that has contributed to what has become a more federal nation is the growth of regional political parties. For instance like the consolidation of parties like the Dravida Munnetra Kazagam (DMK) and the All India Anna Dravidra Munnetra Kazagam (AIADMK) in Tamil Nadu, the Telugu Desam Party (TDP) in Andhra Pradesh amongst others. These parties are based exclusively in the state of the founding, and yet wield national clout by virtue of the seats within Lok Sabha (lower house comprising elected members of parliament) that they hold which in turn might result in them being part of coalition governments at the central level.

---

[25] Mahendra P Singh, "Reorganisation of States in India" 43 (11) *Economic and Political Weekly* (Mar. 15-21, 2008) p 74.

[26] Ibid.

The most important factor that has contributed to the growth of federalism in India has been the jurisprudence carved out by the Supreme Court. As Singh writes faced with the repeated dissolution of state governments by the centre under Article 356 of the Constitution the Supreme Court intervened in a most dramatic fashion.[27] Article 356 of the Constitution provides that if the President upon receipt of a report from the Governor is satisfied that the government of the state cannot be carried in accordance with the constitution, then he/she may essentially suspend the power of the state government and the state legislature and take over those powers and functions. The President under the Constitution symbolically stands for the government comprising the members of the cabinet and the Prime Minister. The President can only act as per the advice of the cabinet and the Prime Minister. Therefore, this provision was much abused by the party or parties in power at the centre to often dispossess state governments of their position. Singh highlights of the more egregious examples of this trend, when he writes of the disbanding of nine Congress governments by the Janata Party in 1977 and in retaliation by the Congress, of nine Janata and other non-Congress governments in 1980.[28]

In response to what was by the early 1990s of a well-established practice by central governments of infringing on the existence of state governments, the Supreme Court in *SR Bommai and Others* v. *Union of India*, ruled that the President can only dissolve a state legislature when such action has been approved by both houses of Parliament, ie the Rajya Sabha and the Lok Sabha. [29] The court also held that the 'satisfaction of the President' is subject to judicial review – meaning that the Supreme Court can look into the materials on which the President relied on to arrive at the conclusion that Article 356 shall be imposed on a state.[30]Further, the court also declared that if proclamation is held to be invalid then the court can hold that the 'status quo ante be restored.'[31]

---

[27] See Mahendra P Singh, "Reorganisation of States in India" 43 (11) *Economic and Political Weekly* (Mar. 15-21, 2008) , p.74.

[28] Ibid.

[29] (1994) 3 SCC 1. See also Mahendra P Singh, "Reorganisation of States in India" 43 (11) *Economic and Political Weekly* (Mar. 15-21, 2008), pp.70-75

[30] Ibid.

[31] Ibid.

Conclusion

The constitution drafters clearly did not envisage the resurgence of the powers of the states that has been witnessed post –independence in India. The drafters that were motivated by the lessons of the demands for separate identities by the various princely states prior to independence worked hard to craft a unitary form of government with the trappings of a federation. Post the adoption of the constitution given the growth of regional parties, the demands of coalition politics and the actions of a resurgent Supreme Court states have emerged as having far more autonomy than was envisaged by the constitutional design. This has also lent incentive to many movements pressing for the recognition and carving out of new states. These demands have been made on the basis of separate language or ethnicity- essentially identity based challenges. Such demands whittle down the most basic constitutional premise of a union that is not based on individual state based identities but of one Bharat that is a union first and a federation later. By not curtailing or prohibiting constitutional amendments in the text the drafters left space for numerous amendments minor and major that have successfully enabled a more conventionally federal country. The Supreme Court concerned by the wanton dissolution of state legislatures by different central governments has put in place protections against such impetuous and politically motivated but constitutionally flawed behaviour. Yet, whether the stronger identities and political powers of states benefits or harms the union is a question that persists? The experience with Princely states in the past seems to indicate that it is a tendency that challenges a strong Union.

Nepal as a Federal State: Lessons From India's Experiences

Lok Raj Baral

Derived from the Latin word *'foederis'* which means 'by contract or treaty', federalism has recently gone into the imagination of the Nepali people. In actual practice however, federalism is ordinarily understood as the distribution of powers and resources between the centers, regional and local units. Independent decision making institutions at various levels are created for addressing the grievances that they have had been deprived of power, resources and opportunities by centralized unitary state. Federalism is also based on" self-rule and shared rule", as Elazar points out, because in democracy, these two principles should be vindicated[1]. Multiple identities based on language, culture, region, or on broad form of ethnicity prompt the political elites to opt for federalism. From a broad Nepali context where social, economic and regional disparities are glaring, the spirit of federalism is also connected to the empowerment of general people. The concept and practice of inclusive democracy and distributive justice is also embedded in the federal model of development. Federalism in other contexts might not be the necessary precondition for achieving these objectives.

Nepal is not yet a federal state; it is likely to be federal under a new constitution to be made in the future. However, all political parties, but one, have committed themselves to making Nepal a federal republic as it has become a fait accompli in the agenda of restructuring of state. The constituent Assembly has also made progress in identifying some basics for carving out the federal units. The High Level State Restructuring Commission

---

[1] Daniel J.Elazar, *Exploring Federalism*, (Tucaloosa, The University of Alabama Press: 1991)

formed by the government further worked on the basis of the Constituent Assembly (CA) committee's Report, though the two conflicting opinions sharply dominated the working of the Commission with the majority members (six) recommending the ten plus one (non- territorial for Dalits) federal units based on both identity and capacity, while the minority (three) opposed identity based units and instead presented its own dissenting view before the government[2]. Politicized as they were, each side including the polarized parties stuck to their guns making federalism as one of the most controversial and crucial agendas of Constitution making. Since the country is already divided into *Ekal Pahichan* (single identity) and plural identity debates, putting political parties along these lines, it greatly affected the CA that ended its life on May 27, 2012 without accomplishing the task of constitution making. Now uncertainty prevails in the midst of intra-party and inter-party conflicts. Why and how Nepal needs federal structure? What compulsions led the political forces to embrace the agenda of federalism in a country whose unitary centralized system and its norms were uninterruptedly practiced since the days of unification of Nepal in the eighteen century?

Unitary system was suitable model in the given geographical situation, power structure, lack of public awareness, patron-client relationship between the rulers and the ruled and above all long period of socialization in subject political culture that made the people Raiti or *Duniyadars* whose share in politics was nil. Only with the end of Rana rule in 1951, semblance, not substance, of democratic exercise was introduced even while keeping Palace - centric politics enact. Ironically, however, with the abolition of monarchy, such a system has continued, despite commitments made occasionally for inclusive and decentralized democracy.

Product of Movement and Complexity

The opinion of making Nepal a federal state was first raised by some Terai leaders in the 1950s, and again in the 1980s when *Nepal Sadbhawana Council* (Nepal Sadbhawana Parishad) was formed by the late Gajendra

---

[2] *See Rajya Punarshamrachana Sujhab Ucchastariya Ayogko Sujhab Pratibedan- 2068* (Report of Recommendation of High level State Restructuring Commission, 2012) (Lalitpur, Nepal: Kathmandu: High level commission for Restructuring of State, 2012)

Narayan Singh. But such demand was interpreted by the ruling elites including the political leaders mostly dominated by the Hill upper caste Brahmins and Chhetris as a threat to national unity and integrity. Meanwhile, the Maoist leaders capitalized the issue of exploitation of Hill ethnic groups, dalits, gender (Mahila) and the Teraiby certain Hill caste groups during the later phase of insurgency in order to enlist the support of these and other poverty stricken segments of population. But the Communist Party of Nepal (Maoist) did not clearly declare Nepal a federal state and instead went for declaring nine autonomous regions based mainly on ethnicity. Only two regions in the mid- and Far West where homogeneous upper caste population has domination were identified as non-ethnic regions. Later, the CPN (Maoist) added two more ethnic based regions.

The clear-cut agenda of federalism came with the Madhesh movement launched in reaction to the failure of the Interim Constitution to include federalism. The whole Terai was shaken by this movement involving all Madhesis including those belonging to different political parties on the plea that these parties had also ignored the issue of Terai. The movement was successful for establishing a new Madhesi identity and power hitherto suppressed for more than two hundred years. The centrality of Kathmandu was challenged and a new Terai nationalism (sub-nationalism) suddenly gets into national politics. As a result, conceding the demands of the Madhesi movement, the Interim Government headed by the Nepali Congress leader, G.P. Koirala, entered into an agreement with the Madhesi leaders. [3] One of the major demands so far unresolved, relates to making the whole of Terai (Madhesh) as one single Pradesh (region).

It seemed that all political parties were caught unaware when the Madhesh movement peaked its momentum with a demand of federalism. Taking it as a clue, other ethnic and regional groups also started demanding autonomous regions on the basis of identity symbolized by language, culture,

---

[3] See the text of Agreement signed between Government of Nepal and Madhesi janaadhikar Forun on 2064/05/13 (VS). Later, the Government of Nepal and the United Madhese Democratic Front or Samyukta Loktantrik Madhesi Morcha consisting of three newly formed parties – Sadbhawana party, Madhesi Janadhikar Forum and Tarai-Madhesh Loktantrik Party - concluded an eight point agreement clarifying various issues pertaining to representation of the Madhesi in security agencies, political power structure and fulfillment of Madhese aspiration for creating autonomous regions. See the Text signed by G.P. Koirala, Prime Minister, and the three Madhesi leaders on 2064/11/16 (VS).

history and long territorial identity etc. Along with such demands also came the problem of carving out autonomous regions on the basis of ethnic identities. The non-Brahmin-Chhetri communities are dispersed across the country. So even if a federal province is created along ethnic line, in Kirat autonomous region, for example, both the Rai and Limbu constitute 48 percent, while the other hill caste and groups constitute 51.8 percent. Linguistically, the population of Rai and Limbu is 29.4 percent, while the Nepali language speaking people constitute 57.4 percent. It has been said that only six districts, out of 75, have larger size of population. In the Bheri-Karnali of the Far Western regions, Brahmin-Chhetri constitutes 67.5 percent, dalit 12.5 percent and other groups 12.9 percent. So is the case in Seti-Mahakali region, the hill Brahmin/Chhetri constitute 85.7 percent, dalit 14.2 percent and 98.3 percent speak Nepali language. Thus, the sound basis of the division of federal units is not yet found despite a lot of opinion being floated from various quarters.

Two main aspects – identity and capacity – have been highlighted by both the Restructuring of the State Committee of CA and the Commission for the Restructuring of State (considered to be an expert commission). The Commission has set aside the prior rights to be granted to the indigenous ethnic groups but has accepted the proportionate representation of ethnic groups in each province and territorial representation (non-ethnic) in provincial administration. Both the Committee and Commission have also underlined the following points: Nepali along with other local languages as official languages; right to self-determination for promotion and protection of culture, language and heritage etc [not for secession] to be allowed to Madhesi and other ethnic groups. The two members of the Commission presented their dissenting opinion supporting the same rights to be granted to the Aryan-Khas group also. Access to natural resources as first right should be granted not only to the indigenous communities but also to the local community[4].

---

[4] Krishna Hachhethu, who was a member of the State Restructuring Commission, has written a series of article clarifying the much muddled issue of identity (pahichan) and ethnic based federalism. See " Prastabit Sanghiyata : Jatiya ki Gair Jatiya" (Proposed Federalism: Ethnic or Non-Ethnic ?), Kantipur, March 25, 2012.

Language, culture, territory, capacity are identified for determining the basis of federal provinces. However, there have been strong reservations for ethnic – based federalism as vociferously demanded by the ethnic, Madhesi and Tharus. The hill ethnic groups and Tharus , who do not like to be identified as Madhesis, had formed a caucus in the CA (now dissolved) in order to put enough pressure to accept ethnic based federalism, although their interpretation of ethnic based federalism is not *Jatiyata* "that deprived other non-ethnic groups of sharing power and resources. According to them, they want to show their identity by naming the provinces on ethnic line. The CA committee has recommended 14 provinces, while the majority members of the Commission have recommended 10+1 (including one non-territorial province for the dalits) and the minority members (three) opted for six as the latter didn't accept the "ethnic-based" provinces. The dissenters felt that ethnic based federalism would disintegrate the nation. It is interesting to note that even the majority members who have been criticized for recommending ethnic based (translated as *jatiyata)* claim that they in fact have also tried to maintain a balance between identity and capability of regional units. In their opinion, the ten provinces appear to be ethnic but in reality they accept plural identity allowing all people to enjoy the same privileges and rights as any other ethnic community.

In Nepal, the federalism debate has deviated from its main objective of self and shared rule. All the stake holders are polarized into two camps - single identity based and plural identity based provinces. Resources and capacity are thus marginalized. Such polarized debates and position taken by various parties also affected the drafting of constitution by the CA thus leading to its dissolution on May 27, 2012.

As in India, the CA in Nepal has also shown its concern about maintaining unity and territorial integrity of the country. No right to self-determination for secession has been granted to any community and regions, nor are unlimited prior rights accepted. Economic viability and administrative feasibility is also taken into account. The CA committee has prepared an elaborate list of distribution of resources and power between Center and lower level units, especially provinces, but the Commission has recommended only two layers –center and provinces—leaving out the local units. The CA committee recommends the creation of special zone *(bishesh chhetra)*, and protected (*Samrakhshit Chhetra)* zone besides local tiers, district and village, for safeguarding the interests of smaller communities whose numbers do not cross one percent. Its rationale is that since provinces cannot be carved out in their names, their rights and privileges need to be protected by making special provisions in the constitution.

Nepal's idea of federalism is not yet crystallized as the major parties and stake holders have not reached a negotiated settlement to the basis of creating provincial units. However, going by the report of CA, it can be stated that Nepal, like India, is likely to adopt centralized federalism in which the Center will have political, financial and residual powers. Indian constitution has not mentioned the word federal. The makers of Indian constitution considered that India is a "conglomerate of numerous minorities placed along side an uncaring and orthodoxy-ridden caste Hindu majority"[5]. Due to the spirit of integration of various former princely states, India is known as the "union of states" because it was imperative that the reorganization of state boundaries was drawn on the basis of linguistic, historic, literary and cultural diverse regions of India.

Indian Experience

Indian federal system is not similar to the US system because of the former's emphasis on the role of Center. Recognizing the ethno-linguistic territorial identities, states were created. Now other criteria are also adopted that do not explicitly rely on ethno-linguistic basis. Constitutional experts working on India have a kind of unanimous view on the centralized character, despite a variety of narratives provided by them. K.C. Wheare's "quasi-federalism", Ivor Jennings's description of India ' as a federation with a strong centralizing tendency' are in common to show the central features in the Indian federal system. Articles 356 and 360 have categorically made it a centralized federalism as the President of India, on the advice of the Council of Ministers, can declare national emergency on the grounds of the reasons stipulated in the articles - war, financial crisis, constitutional breakdown etc. Under such circumstances, all powers of state would be suspended.

---

[5] J.K. Bajaj, "Towards a Review of the Indian Constitution" in Prof. R,N. Pal, ed., *Indian Constitutional Review* (Chandigarh: CRRID, 2002),p.32.

Similarly, there are a number of financial aspects that make the states more dependent on the Center. The Planning Commission has also major role to dole out funds for the states and in crisis situation making the state governments look upon the Center for salvaging them from financial difficulties.

Any federal system in the developing countries is subject to newer demands coming from its federal constituencies and hence it becomes dynamics, while at the same time retaining the basics of the constitutional spirit. The Constitution Review Committee set up by the Vajpayee Government in 1999 seemed to know the grievances of states vis-à-vis the center. Thus, centralized federal spirit alone cannot address the emerging trends of center-state relations. Both 'bargaining' and 'cooperative' federal spirit need to be examined, given the shifting political scenarios in the country. Yet, federalism means cooperation and accommodation for insuring shared and self rule.

The Indian states get essential prerequisites for development. Rural development, health, education, medical and public health facilities , welfare of the Scheduled castes and Scheduled Tribes, roads building and other kinds of infrastructure building activities. In short, it can be said that except defense, Finance, Foreign Affairs, Home, Trade and Commerce, Nuclear development etc., all other functions needed for the development of states are allotted to them. Nevertheless, the Indian constitution is heavily weighed in favour of the Centre because of its control over a number of important areas including the financial resources. The Gadgil Formula, (1991-1992), has made the following criteria for allocation of financial assistance to individual states:

(a) population : 60 percent;

(b) per capita state domestic product below the national average : 25 percent;

(c) per capita tax efforts of state : 7.5 percent; and

(d) special problems: 7.5 percent.

The National Development Council makes adjustments from time to time. The Sarkaria Commission made 247 recommendations in all emphasizing the functional relations between the Union and states. Since India has three list of functions for the Union and states. First is Central list in which some crucial areas as identified before are included. The next is state list in which the allocation of functions to be carried out by the states is listed. The third is concurrent list that needs to be discharged by both the Center and states. Sometimes, some of the functions allotted to states are also used by the Union government. "Theoretically, both the Union and states can legislate on this list, but Parliamentary legislation suspends state legislation. For all practical purposes, the third list is a Union List". So the spirit of the Indian constitution is unitary rather than federal[6].

India's political landscape has undergone a change since the end of one-party dominant system in the late 1960s. The Indian National Congress is no more the single dominant party; nor can it alone run the central government without the cooperation of and alliance formation with other regional parties. So survival has become the first priority of any central government now days and if the largest party (not majority party) is short of votes in Parliament even for passing a bill , it needs to court the small regional parties. One of the most recent examples was the role of one of the alliance partners of the Congress that put up conditions for support of Presidential candidate. Despite being a member of the United Democratic Alliance (UDA), the Trinamool Congress chief was reluctant to extend support to the Presidential candidate who came from her own state, West Bengal. She wanted to get adequate central aid for bailing out her state from debt. It can thus be called some kind of a bargaining federalism with which state governments try to get benefits, though such strategies may not always work.

Nevertheless, it must be admitted that Indian federal system has matured a lot in recent years. Unlike the strained center-state relations that often led the Center to dismiss state governments, no central government has

---

[6] See Ranjit Singh Ghuman, Inderjeet Singh, " Socio-Economic Change and Development under the Constitution: A Retrospection", Ibid.,p.104 and 106.

resorted to such steps for over two decades. Opposition parties in state governments are comfortable with the Center demonstrating that cooperative federalism is now on sound footing.

Lessons for Nepal

India is federal both by design and evolution. The 1935 Act based on diarchy had prepared grounds for constitution. The diarchy system was reformulated, improved and elaborated along with the integration of princely states. The process of making a constitution was smooth because of Indian political leaders who had got their apprenticeship in some sort of a democratic exercise during the British Raj. And to the credit of Indian leaders, who were visionary and pragmatic, Indian federal structure has continued and it depends on the success story of Indian parliamentary democracy. The Indian states complain against the center for not allocating them adequate funds for developmental purposes, but they have not gone against it to the extent of disintegration of the nation itself. The strong center has been able to hold all of them together. Some states in the Northeast are perennially embroiled in insurgencies but the Indian state has either contained them or managed to resolve the problems. For such containment requires central resources, capacity, power and political ingenuity. And India has, as of now, been able to use all of them in order to maintain the national unity and territorial integrity of the country.

Nepal's case is different from India's. First, Nepal has not yet become a federal state despite some ground works done about it. Some basic issues such as the basis of creating federal units has to be cleared with the understanding and cooperation of all people demanding regional units. Harmonization of opinion on this issue is a must before we venture into the domain of federalism.

Indian democratic system has been more or less successful along with great difficulties encountered by it in its historical trajectory. Rampant corruption, threats of terrorism, politics of violence and criminalization and weakening parties at the national level plus its spending on defence etc. have put strains in the system. Its gigantic problems cannot be compared with Nepal in magnitude and in intensity. But Nepal's problems loom large when the core political elites of Nepal fail to acknowledge the gravity of the situation. Nepal has not yet settled the issue of a political system, let alone the issue of making it a federal state.

Political landscape of Nepal is more problematic than India's. Parties are being fragmented; leaders seem to be losing their credibility and capacity for engaging different communities and regional groupings. So the nation state is adrift. Nepal has therefore to grapple with many problems at a time – political instability, crisis of governance and lack of political direction and development. Meanwhile, foreign concern about the pro and cons of federalism in Nepal is increasing because of Nepal's own failure to assure its neighbours and others that federal Nepal would not at all prove. As the press reports go, China seems to be worried about creating more autonomous regions in the Hills as these units, in its view, may be detrimental to its security in Tibet. However, such anxiety can be removed by strong commitment to be made by the major parties assuring them that federal Nepal would in no circumstances jeopardize the security interests of Nepal's immediate neighbours. Moreover, federalism, in the given situation, has become a reality for distribution of power and resources. As it has gone much beyond the proposal of decentralization of power, only a federal structure which is acceptable to all Nepalis may resolve the problem.

Federalism, Foreign policy and National Security in Nepal: Lessons From Neighbourhood

"Federalism and spirited foreign policy go ill together"
K. G. Wheare[1]

Nepal's nascent debate on federalism is more centered on identity politics than on its implications on foreign policy and national security. There is not enough discussion as to what type of federalism is suited in view of Nepal's geopolitical location and geostrategic interests. Neither is there any constructive debate as to how Nepal's neighbours are watching their interests in the context of discussion on federalism that is being introduced in Nepal and how they will respond to the new federal set up. As a country sandwiched between two geographic, economic, and demographic giants of Asia poised to be new powerhouses of the world, Nepal cannot remain oblivious in its federal discourse of the tremendous political and economic shift that is taking place in both countries, especially in Nepal's neighbouring states and provinces. The issues of federalism in Nepal are inextricably linked with foreign policy and national security, on which Nepal can learn a lot from the experiments and experience in its neighbourhood. Federalism may bring about new opportunities in addressing the existing inequalities and gaps among geographic regions and ethnic groups. But it may complicate the issues related to foreign policy and national security, unless the questions are properly addressed beforehand.

---

[1] K C Wheare, *Federal Government*, 4th edition, (London: Oxford University Press; 1963)

Lesson I: States or provinces in a federal set up will have a say in foreign policy, no matter how the constitution is framed

In a federal set up, foreign policy is often cited as the classic example of tasks that is placed under the sole responsibility of the central government, for it relates to issues of sovereignty, territorial integrity, and conduct of relations with foreign countries. In political and foreign policy literature, there is almost unanimity that the jurisdiction on foreign affairs should rest with the centre and any interests and concerns of the states should be addressed through a supremacy clause in the constitution that empowers the centre to have the final say. This is also justified by the uniformity argument, i.e. only the centre can devise uniform response on issues of national interest in relation to foreign affairs.

Even if the constitution of a country is explicit about the exclusive jurisdiction of the centre on foreign policy and national security issues, the states will have interests and influences over them. In a federal set up, the states will seek to benefit from space in foreign policy ("desire for free lunch") as long as it in their interest and it is freely available to them. It has been an obvious lesson from around the region, including in India, that the states will exercise much influence in foreign policy, no matter how the constitution is framed. Although foreign policy is the exclusive domain of the central government, states in India are increasingly asserting their influence because of the increasing role of regional parties in coalition government in the centre. Since the 1990s, the liberalization of economic policy allowed increased leverage to the Indian state governments to negotiate the terms of foreign investment in their states, especially in the case of energy and agriculture negotiations[2]. Lately, the Indian vote against Sri Lanka in the Human Rights Council in 2011 on the latter's handling of war against Tamil Tigers was a case of strong assertion from political blocs in Tamil Nadu over the central government, of which they are coalition partners. Similarly, the recent reluctance to allow the U.S. retail giant Wal-Mart to open up stores in India has to do with strong opposition from West Bengal's ruling party, which is part of coalition in the central government.

---

[2] KripaSridharan, 'Federalism and Foreign Relations: The Nascent Role of the Indian States', *Asian Studies Review*, 27(4): 463-89., 2003

The rise of coalition politics at the centre has resulted into a "paradigm shift" in the centre-state relations in India[3], leading to much bigger stake and influence of the states in the conduct of foreign policy.

In the new federal set up in Nepal, it must be assumed that new provinces or states- to- be will have a say on foreign policy matters, even if the constitution puts exclusive jurisdiction of foreign policy under the central government. The provinces will exercise it through articulation of their interests on cross-border ethnicity of populations, movement of goods, services and people along the border, attraction of foreign investment in the respective provinces, issues of citizenship, and cross-border crime etc. There must be institutionalized mechanism to address such interests and concerns of the provinces in a new federal set up, so it does not become a permanent source of centre-state conflict and tensions.

In India, it has also been observed that regional political parties exert greater extra-constitutional influence in foreign policy when they are not part of coalition at the centre[4]. It is quite likely that regional political parties are better equipped to influence the foreign policy from within, when they are part of the coalition in the centre. In view of their relative significance in national politics and economy, the provinces in Nepal's Terai can also exert extra-constitutional influence in foreign policy. This factor cannot be ignored while considering foreign policy during the federalization of the country. In such situation when the states start challenging the centre's authority, a backlash from the centre may not only harm the centre-state relations, but it can also affect the relations with a foreign country.

Lesson II: Various constitutional instruments can be applied in addressing the overlapping interests between the states and the centre in a federal set up

Major foreign policy issues such as establishment and maintenance of

---

[3] William J. Antholis paper presented at a seminar on "Understanding Federalism and Foreign Policy in India and China", 16 January, 2012, IIT Madras China Study Centre,

[4] Dossani, Rafiq and VijaykumarSrinidhi , "Indian Federalism and the Conduct of Foreign Policy in Border States: State Participation and Central Accommodation since 1990", *Domestic Politics and Indian Foreign Policy*, A. Mattoo and H Joseph (eds), New Delhi: Routledge, www.stanfod.edu

diplomatic relations, signing and ratification of treaties and control of boundary falls within the exclusive jurisdiction of the federal government. But there are other issues related to foreign policy and national security where the states will want to have a say. Such issues include issues of ethnic, religious and linguistic interests on either side of the border, interest in share and exploitation of natural resources, movement of people, services and goods across the border, and in security such as border security, cross-border crime and extremism and terrorism.

Usually, the overlapping jurisdiction on foreign policy related matter between the centre and the states is resolved through four constitutional instruments. First, the provision of concurrent list such as in the Constitution of India, which lists subjects on which state and centre have overlapping responsibilities. Second, the parliamentary supremacy of centre, which can resolve issues of conflicting claims of jurisdiction. Third, again as in the Indian constitution, the concept of residual power, which rests with the centre. Fourth, the constitution can insert a foreign policy preemption clause, which precludes the states from making any legislation on foreign policy-related matters, something found in the United States' constitution, which gives supremacy to federal laws over state laws. These points have strong relevance and should be taken into consideration while designing federalism in the country.

Besides, there may be issues which may not have direct foreign policy implications, but can have externalities that need to be addressed jointly. Positive externalities such as the sister-city arrangements, opening of chambers of state business and industry, cultural connections etc. are supposed to deliver positive relations. But negative externalities, such as creating liabilities on account of certain legislation of regulation, cases such as in WTO rules on environmental standards, property rights and agriculture issues, might affect the relations with a foreign country, the consequences of which has to be borne by the centre. For such issues, the process of legal arbitration on obligations created by the states will have to be devised in the constitution.

Lesson III: There is no single model of federalism that can be applied in Nepal as a template for addressing the identity question

The issue of federalism was the principal source of disagreement in the constitution-making process in Nepal. Failure of Nepal's first elected Constituent Assembly (CA) to adopt a new constitution before its unceremonial demise on 28 May 2012 owes primarily to its inability to articulate a compromise on the issue of state restructuring, mainly on the issue of federalism- the principal difference being the polarization on choosing an identity model. A main cause of polarization was whether the restructuring would be done along single-identity-based states or if the new federal states would have neutral or multiethnic identity in their names. Though the first sitting of the elected assembly declared the country as a "federal democratic republic", it was not clear as to what would be the model of federalism to be adopted. The two separate processes under the Constituent Assembly endorsed the single-identity states separately, but recommended different names and numbers of provinces[5]. The Maoists, the Madhesi and the federation of Janajatis, who had membership across major parties, supported single-identity states, while Nepali Congress and other traditional parties would only accept multi-ethnic identity. Even after the dissolution of the Constituent Assembly, the ruling Maoists and Madhesi have announced a "federalist alliance" together with the Janajatis, who have also declared their intention to form a political party of their own. Others have opposed single identity-model of federalism, making consensus even more difficult. Successful conclusion of any constitutional compact that may emerge now will hinge upon the success of debate on federalism in the country, especially on choosing an identity model on which the political discourse is highly polarized.

There is no single prescription model on federalism that can be replicated in Nepal, while two common models have relevance to foreign policy and national security. In vertical federalism, the centre retains substantive and

---

[5] In January 2010, a report of the Committee on Restructuring of the State and Distribution of Power (CRSPD) of the CA recommended 14 autonomous provinces along single-identity model and the report of the High-Level Commission on State Restructuring (2011) recommended 10 states, also on single identity.

exclusive authority on certain issues, including foreign policy. Vertical federalism seeks to impose uniformity in response of states to foreign affairs though superimposing role of the centre on foreign policy matters. Horizontal federalism allows states some regulatory powers that may affect foreigners in relation to their movement (immigration), business (trade and investment), which entails uniformity and coordination problems.

Thus the principle roadblock ahead is the choice among different models federalism, mainly between single-identity versus multiple-identity or identity-neutral federalism. Since this has already taken the form of identity politics, some kind of relations with identity in naming the provinces, be it ethnic, cultural, linguistic, or geographic, cannot be denied. In India, the federal states have adopted names of mixed ethnic, linguistic, regional or geographic identity. In India, the mixed identity model applying nationality (Bengal, Punjab, Tamil Nadu) and regional identity (Uttar Pradesh, Madhya Pradesh etc.) have worked relatively well. Such a mixed model, though highly relevant in Nepal's context, may not satisfy the aspirations of identity of Nepal's Madhesi, Janajatis and other marginalized and excluded groups. In Pakistan, the federally administered tribal areas (FATA) provide unique model, but they are not without problems. These models will have relevance to Nepal, though they are not easily replicable.

Lesson IV: Dispelling fear of backlash and alienation with or without federalism will be an important challenge

One of the critical challenges in Nepal's federalism debate is the fear of backlash and alienation of some groups if their interests are compromised. There is apprehension among some political parties and non-ethnic groups that "single-identity federalism", which they discount as "ethnic federalism", will be a divisive political issue which, according to them, will undermine Nepal's long standing social harmony and national unity. They also claim that it will pose a security threat and jeopardize Nepal's external relations with neighbouring countries, which have overlapping populations along the either side of border with similar ethnic, linguistic and cultural backgrounds. Even academic write-ups suggest that "ethnic federalism" will be inappropriate for Nepal[6]. There is no guarantee however, that ethnic conflict will not surface if the grievances of the diverse ethnic groups and traditionalized groups are left unaddressed in the new constitution. In the past, the Maoist People's War sought to assert this issue violently, for example.

If single-identity-based federal states are agreed upon, there are dangers of backlash from the mainstream high-caste and non-ethnic people. In the wake of dissolution of the Constituent Assembly in May 2012, the Bahun and Chhetri groups had already staged nation-wide protests asking separate recognition for each in the constitution and opposing the single-ethnic model of federalism, as did the people of the far-western region and the Muslims. The ethnic coalition of Janajatis and Tharus launched separate agitations asking for single-identity states.

One of the key challenges in choosing a model of federalism lies in the equation of mutually exclusive demands of various groups. The demands put forward by various groups across the nation are mutually exclusive. In other words, if demands made by certain groups are accepted, others will be losers. For example, Tharus want a separate province of their own (tharuhat), whereas the Madhesi want them to be under the part of Madhesh and the people in the far-western districts want them to be part of undivided far-west (akhandsudurpaschim). Similarly, the Terai plains of eastern Nepal in Mechi zone are claimed by the Limbuan movement, the single Madhesh claimers and those seeking a separate Kochila state. In such situation, creating a win-win for all is a big challenge, which requires a lot of political maturity, wisdom and pragmatism, which is a rare commodity in the present day Nepal.

Nepal cannot afford to create federal states for each of 118 ethnic groups in the country. Other marginalized groups such as women, Dalits, Muslims and smaller minorities may feel further alienated and marginalized, as their concerns cannot be addressed through federalism alone. Such marginalization might create losers and those seeking to assert their identity fuelling the demands for creation of more ethnic states in a "domino effect" until the demands of all groups are satisfied. In India, the case of violence

---

[6] Dev Raj Dahal and YubarajGhimire, "Ethnic Federalism in Nepal: Risks and Opportunities", *Georgetown Journal of International Affairs*, Vol 13, No. 1, Winter/Spring 2012

in the Bodo territories and displacement of Muslim populations in some of districts of Assam, northeastern provinces of India and the latest spread of violence in to other places since July 2012 is a case in point. Allegation of the Indian authorities against elements from a foreign country and asking to lift malicious postings on social networking shows how such domino effect will be difficult to handle.

Lesson V: Poor financial viability may lead to unleashing of unhealthy competition among the provinces for allocation of resources, foreign aid and foreign direct investment

In the United States, creative federalism was applied since the 1960s through channeling grant from the federal government for the social programs in states. Though that may sound to be too centralized and patronizing, centre's support towards financial sustainability of the states will be an inevitable question in a federal set up. This was somewhat superseded by Ronald Reagan's new federalism, which sought to reduce the federal grant to states. In Nepal, it is conceivable that most Nepali federal provinces will need massive support from the centre, at least for a period of time, in order to sustain themselves financially. Such dependence upon the centre on resources may unleash unhealthy competition for allocation of resources, including in channeling of foreign aid and investment. In India, channeling of foreign aid may not be an issue, but there is a strong competition for attracting foreign direct investment in the states.

Viability of new provinces in a federal set up will be important in view of internal harmony as well as foreign policy. While the principal aim of federalism is to making the local government's capable of owing and executing their own priorities, the limited natural resource distribution makes them dependent on the centre. As more resources will be required in the newly created states to meet the expectations to cater to the needs of socioeconomic development, their dependence upon foreign assistance will be further entrenched and will siphon the already weak tax-base available for the central as well as provincial governments. This debate of capacity, left unanswered so far, will remain an important issue ahead, as most of Nepal's revenue is currently collected from only three districts, including the capital. India's Finance Commission has done the job of allocating resources to states relatively well without much controversy. Nepal can learn from there. Issue of capacity of states or provinces is likely to impact the sustainability of federalism, as creation of states with low capacity almost certainly leads to a strong central government, which defies the purpose of federalism as the division of power between the centre and the periphery.

Foreign policy is best managed when there is cooperative federalism, i.e. when the states cooperate with each other and with the centre as a mutually complimentary part of a single governmental mechanism, without challenging the centre's authority on foreign affairs. The Indian model of federalism, especially in relation to foreign policy, has been described as "cooperative" federalism[7]. Except in rare cases of extra-constitutional influence becoming evident in the context of rise of regional blocs and coalition politics at the centre, Indian states work on a cooperative federalism model, especially in foreign policy matters. In cases of competitive federalism, where the states are in competition with the centre, the domain of foreign policy becomes weak and results into several problems. Competitive federalism is not necessarily a wrong thing, as it encourages competition among states on issues like attracting investment and businesses. As competition applies mostly over allocation of power and resources, they are bound to have influences in foreign policy.

One of the major perils of federalism in relation to foreign policy is the danger of friction among the federal government and state governments on the issues that relates with foreign policy matters, especially with neighbours. For example, a state bordering a neighbouring country may choose to block water discharge of a river downstream to another country contrary to the treaty obligations and wish of the central government, if the interests of the state in question are undermined. West Bengal's resistance to discharge agreed level of the water to Bangladesh as per the Ganges Treaty (1996) speaks of such possibilities. Such friction may also arise in the negotiation of issues of exploitation of other natural resources. Unless clearly defined,

---

[7] J AntholisWilliam, *Understanding Federalism and Foreign Policy in India and China*, Paper presented on16 January 2012, at IIT Madras

the role of states becomes obvious in negotiation with foreign governments on the execution of big power or infrastructure projects located in the states, in which foreign assistance is involved. Similar complexity might also arise in attracting foreign investment in certain states, which may consider it their prerogative, whereas the central movement might still want to have a say on such matters.

Lesson VI: Federalism cannot be built in one day

One of the significant lessons from our neighbourhood is building federalism requires a lot of time. Failure to recognize this cardinal principle led to failure of Nepal's first elected Constituent Assembly in writing a new constitution. Even if the constitution provides a strong foundation, federalism is an evolving process. Even after sixty years of federal system, federalism in India has been sometimes described as "work in progress"[8]. In the last six decades and half, several new states have been carved from existing ones. The process was not without problems, as it led to violence, conflict and in some cases prolonged insurgency. India has long history of handling insurgency related to demands of separate states from within states. Even today, India has outstanding questions of identity and new groups asking for their own states or autonomous provinces (e.g. Telangana). There are no quick fixes to question of identity, ethnicity, and geographical and cultural diversity, which federalism alone cannot address. This is the experience learned from other countries in the region.

India is among the countries which has managed federal states with relative success, although the makers of the Indian constitution feared fissiparous tendencies and had devised strong national unity clauses empowering the centre on many counts. Applying a mix of geographic, linguistic and cultural identities, the Indian federal states have effectively sought to address the aspirations of its people without undermining their relations and authority of the central government and the state. In foreign policy, the states are in near perfect harmony, though it has become clearer in recent times that Indian states are increasingly asserting their role in

---

[8] Balveer Arora, India's Experience with Federalism: Lessons Learnt and Unlearnt, paper presented at an international seminar on "Constitutionalism and Diversity in Nepal" on 22-24 August 2007, Kathmandu

foreign policy advocacy and application. This is partly because India gives a strong role for the centre on almost all issues, including on foreign policy. Such heavily skewed power at the hands of central government in India has also been labeled as "quasi-federalism"[9]. In Pakistan, strong central government has weakened the federal system despite strong constitutional foundations.

Lesson VII: Asymmetrical federalism will be difficult to manage

One of the lessons from India is that "asymmetrical federalism" is difficult to manage. For example, despite the special status that India provides to Jammu and Kashmir under Article 370 of the constitution, the issue remains largely unresolved. In Pakistan, Punjab Province alone has more population (55.6%) than the rest of three provinces (Sindh, Baluchistan and NWFP), which has been a source of asymmetry, at times leading to political friction. The special power status of Nepal's provinces-to-be in the Terai, more so if there is "one Madhesh", as is being demanded, will lead to an asymmetrical federalist set up which will have bearing on foreign policy issues[10].

Further, in a federal state power balance may shift from the centre to the states, as has been experienced lately in India. The states in India are not only growing in their significance in economic and political sectors, they are asserting big influence in decision-making and policy-making in foreign policy-related matters. Such influences owes to their increasing their political clout (example West Bengal) and their high economic growth trajectory led by reformist Chief Ministers, such as in the case of Bihar and Gujarat[11]. Such shifting power balance towards states in India, through economic growth in Bihar and increasing political clout of West Bengal and Uttar Pradesh are also likely to count in the new federal set up in Nepal. Similar

---

[9] U C Jain and Jeevan Nair, *Centre-State Relations.* (Jaipur : Pointer Publishers, 2000)

[10] In Terai alone, there is 885 km stretch of border with India and nearly half (48%) of Nepal's population.

[11] Amb. Karl F. Inderfurth and Persis Khambatta, " Indian States: Agents of Change", US-India Insight Newsletter, Centre for Strategic and International Studies, Vol. 2, No 8, August 2012, available online at http://csis.org/files/publication/120814_India _States_Agents_Change.pdf

rise in influence of Nepal's provinces in the Terai is likely to be important economically, but can be challenging politically in a federal set up, in which several hill provinces will have to depend upon the Terai provinces on a number of counts.

One of the principal foreign policy concerns in a federal set up in Nepal will be that of uniformity in responding the foreign countries or neighbouring states of foreign countries by several Nepali states. As of now, Nepal has borders with Indian states of Uttaranchal, Uttar Pradesh, Bihar, West Bengal and Sikkim as well as with Tibet autonomous region of China. It is conceivable that almost all of the states proposed by all formulations will at least have a foreign country in its boundary. Each state or province will have an external boundary, which is also a state or province in that country. Handling of boundary and related issues of border security, immigration, movement of populations, goods and services, and issues of cross border crime and security issues will have great bearing on Nepal's foreign relations with its neighbouring countries. Here, Nepal cannot afford to have divergent responses from several states of provinces. Creating uniformity in foreign policy issues from the states or provinces will be a big challenge that needs to be addressed, both in the process of constitution-making and in the conduct of foreign policy.

Lesson VIII: Federalism will raise the need for "constituent diplomacy"

Despite the exclusive jurisdiction of the central government on foreign policy in most countries, there is requirement of consulting with respective states in matters related to the relations with a neighbouring country bordering them. In India, the central government regularly consults the states bordering Nepal on matters related to border security, trade and transit facilities, and immigration issues. The bordering Indian states have direct stake on the central government's negotiations with Nepal on water resources issues, especially on the discharge of rivers and the transmission of power generated from hydropower projects. The increasing role of the states in foreign policy and its management, commonly called as "constituent diplomacy"[12] is a common feature in federal set up, especially where there is a strong democratic constitution which allows greater debate and discussion. This is common in many countries, and is increasingly a practice in India. Under a federal set up, Nepal will have to engage in such "constituent diplomacy", mostly with bordering states of neighbouring countries, mainly in the Terai. During unitary set up, Nepal had discouraged opening foreign consulates in regional cities and commercial hubs. Only an Indian consulate was allowed in Birgunj after the operationalization of the Inland Container Depot in the city. Similar requests from other countries and in other cities will be irresistible in the context of rising aspiration of the new provinces to be recognized as commercial and economic entities of their own when they enter federal set up.

Lesson IX: Chinese interest on federalism has relevance to Nepal

China espouses unique model on devolution of power and shows exemplary accommodation through such innovation as "one country two systems" that is applicable with regard to Hong Kong, Macao and Taiwan, and to some extent to Tibet Autonomous Region. China allows relative freedom to its provinces to establish its relations with neighbouring countries. Tibet Autonomous Region has extensive contacts and relations with Nepal, which of course is supervised by the Chinese government. Beijing wants Yunnan province to be "gateway" to South and Southeast Asia and allows Kunming local government to contact foreign governments on its own.

China has usually refrained from commenting on Nepal's internal affairs, often repeating its long-standing policy of non-intervention. However, such stance seems to be changing in the context of debate on federalization in Nepal. Traditionally, the Chinese political and security interests in Nepal used to be aimed towards securing support to its "one-China policy" and containing any "anti-China" (read Free Tibet) activities in Nepal, including the influx Tibetan refugees. But in the context of simmering unrest in the Western Chinese provinces, as is demonstrated by waves of Tibetan and other live immolations and the question of Muslim population called Uighurs in Xinxiang, Beijing is viewing the rise of identity politics in Nepal, especially

---

[12] John Kincaid, 'Constituent Diplomacy in Federal Polities and the Nation-state: Conflict and Co-operation' in Hans J. Michelmann and PanyotisSoldatos (eds) *Federalism and International Relations—The Role of Subnational Units*. (Oxford: Clarendon Press, 1990).

in the context of federalism in Nepal, with a lot of caution. It is no surprise that a visiting Chinese foreign ministry official during his May 2012 visit was reportedly as warning the Nepalese political officials of the negative consequences of "ethnic federalism". A newly split Nepalese Maoist party official on his August 2012 visit to China is also reported to have been told of the Chinese concern on the "increasing external influence" on the debate on federalism in Nepal. While this remains to be independently confirmed, it has not been denied by the Chinese either. Any wave of ethnic uprising in neighbouring Nepal is not unlikely to affect the bordering regions of Tibet Autonomous Region, as there are people with similar ethnic, linguistic and religious backgrounds on either side of border between Nepal and China. The flurry of visits of Chinese officials may have to do with increasing Chinese interest to develop ties with Nepal and in the context of its rising economic influence in the region and around the globe. But it is not irrelevant to the ongoing political transformation in Nepal and the discussion on federal restructuring.

Lesson X: Federalism cannot be completed without considering national security

Though national security is also often left in the jurisdiction of the centre, it is often tied with federalism as the states will have critical role related to security. Issues of cross-border crime and terrorism, which may fall in the jurisdiction of central government, cannot be resolved without active involvement and cooperation of the states. Nepal's open and porous border with India allows room for unscrupulous elements, extremists and terrorists to commit crimes in one country and to seek sanctuary in the other. Sometimes, conflicting jurisdiction over the issues of national security between the state and centre may compound these problems. This also brings the question of extradition and mutual legal assistance. Though the centre will have a say in the former, especially in designing bilateral treaty and processes, the role of states and provinces will be crucial in preventing and combating cross-border crime.

Armed outfits in the Terai, which have somewhat remained dormant in recent times, will be an issue of concern, especially in the context their use of territories on either side for gathering arms, training and launching their covert activities. If the new provinces fail to manage the expectations of identity, it may unleash fresh violence of the outfits alarming the neighbouring states, affecting their interest, and enticing their interference. If the new constitution fails to address the Madhesi grievances, the dormant armed groups in Terai might exploit the situation re-launching their activities with demand for "self-determination". Such radicalization of political agenda in the federal Nepal is likely to raise security bars in the neighbouring countries. It is conceivable that ethnic, linguistic, geographic, and to some extent religious mobilization will be there in Nepal for some time to come, as the constitution alone cannot address all the identity-related grievances. Preventing cultural, linguistic, and ethnic polarization in the new federal setting will require a good understanding and cooperation from across the border, where there are populations with commonalities on each count. Nepal's neighbouring countries and their states in particular, will need a politically stable Nepal that will not pose security threat to them and that will not harbor elements inimical to their security interests.

The Maoist movement in Nepal is often said to have inspired the Indian Maoists, who have now succeeded in expanding their movement to several hundred Indian districts[13], creating a red corridor prompting the Indian Prime Minister Manmohan Singh to declare the Maoist insurgency as the India's biggest security threat, even ahead of the issue of militancy in Jammu and Kashmir. This issue will continue to remain a thorny aspect of India's relations with new Nepali provinces bordering Nepal, especially if they are unable to deny safe heaven and supply of weapons to the Indian Maoists from the Nepalese territories.

Nepal's population living in the bordering areas to neighbouring countries, especially India, has a seamless flow, back and forth for social and economic purposes. Nepal's Terai, which accounts for 17% of the country's area and 48% of population, has extensive social contacts, relations and movements with bordering Indian states. Any conflict that may arise

---

[13] Though the number of districts affected by the Indian Maoist Movement has dropped from 223 in 2008 to 182 in 182 in 2011, according to Union Home Ministry, an open source portal (www.satp.org) says that intensity of the Movement has actually increased during the period.

on either side of the border has potential of spilling over to the other side causing concern on foreign affairs, which the bordering states alone cannot handle, arousing security concerns and undermining the friendly relations between the two countries. In such situation, the capacity of the neighbours to support peaceful resolution of the problem becomes blurred, as they may be seen as party to the issue and part of the problem, not part of solution.

In most cases, the jurisdiction over immigration and movement of foreigners across borders is in the exclusive jurisdiction of the centre, though the cooperation of the state officials is a must in execution of the legal and policy provisions made by the centre. In India, the central government has often accused states in the bordering regions to have been "soft" on illegal movement of populations. As there is free movement of people between India and Nepal as per the provisions of 1950 Treaty of Peace and Friendship, softer positions employment in states or provinces on either side may tend to bring tensions between the centre and the states. The question of citizenship, which is one paramount concern to the people of Terai, cannot be the sole prerogative of the central government. How the new provinces or states will handle the distribution of citizenship and how that might arouse the interest from across the border will also be something of a new dimension to handle in the new federal set up. How the provinces will handle the issues of cross-border migration will also be important for national security interests. In the case of China, the centre may want to impose stricter restriction on illegal border-crossing of the Tibetans, whereas the bordering states may want to be appearing softer on humanitarian and cultural grounds.

Lesson XI: Managing external influence on federalism will be a crucial test for Nepal

Regional and international influences will definitely count in adopting a model of federalism. There is a widespread allegation that the identity-based federalism is being supported by Nepal's European donors, who have not done enough to dispel this perception. Similarly, there is unfounded notion that concept of federalism in Nepal was "made in India", taking cue from India's generally supportive position towards of the aspiration of Nepalese people, including that of Terai, for inclusion, more rights and more authority in managing their own affairs through federalism. Managing Indian interest and influence without letting them meddle in Nepal's internal affairs will be an important challenge to handle in the course of federalization and restructuring of the Nepali state. As we have discussed, China is believed to be against any ethnic connotation in fear of ethnic spillover in its Western provinces, mainly its Tibet autonomous region. Thus, the external interest and influence of Nepal's neighbours will be yet another important dimension that Nepal will have to manage in the pursuit of federalism.

New Delhi's role in facilitating the 2005 agreement between the parties and the Maoists has been widely acknowledged. Recent revelations of an Indian Professor that the Maoists had written to the Indian government in 2002 assuring to protect their interest[14] also shows how much India matters in Nepal. How India will approach the issue of federalism in Nepal, especially in the context of Nepal's political parties seeking the Indian support for any consensus building exercise for new constitution of Nepal, will be highly relevant. Influences apart, untying the infamous Gordian Knot of federalism in Nepal may also require some kind of external support, if it continues to be the bone of contention in the political process ahead.

A recent report on India' foreign and strategic policy mentions that India's states have vital stakes in their neighbouring countries (Bengal in Bangladesh; Bihar in Nepal; Punjab in Pakistan; Tamil Nadu in Sri Lanka)[15]. It shows that there is going to be a strong external influence in Nepal's discourse on federalism. The interest in growth zones in Nepal's neighbouring states of India and China, especially in Bihar and Tibet, will also be of tremendous significance to Nepal's newly created provinces or states.

---

[14] Muni S D, "Bringing the Maoists down from the Hills: India's role" in *Nepal in Transition: From People's War to Fragile Peace*, eds. Sebastian von Einsiedel*et. al*, (Cambridge: Cambridge University Press, 2012)

[15] Sunil Khilnani et al., "Nonalignment 2.0: A Foreign and Strategic Policy for India in the Twenty First Century," Centre for Policy Research, Working Paper, January 2012, available online at http://www.cprindia.org/sites/default/files/NonAlignment%202.0_1.pdf

Lesson XII: Federalism alone will not solve all of Nepal's multi-faceted problems. It may complicate foreign policy and national security, unless addressed beforehand.

It has been generally conceived that federalism will bring tremendous opportunities to the traditionally excluded, marginalized and oppressed communities and areas in Nepal, who will be free to release their dormant energy in the new federal set up because of a shift from the so-called "second class citizenship" to that of equal citizens with equal opportunities. While this is partly true, federalism will not solve Nepal's multi-faceted problems.

Though federalism has already been accepted as a mode for state restructuring, Nepalis are sharply divided as to what are the advantages and disadvantages of federalism, and its various models. Some consider federalism to be panacea of Nepal's problem of exclusion and marginalization and friction between the centre and periphery. Others regard it as a Pandora's Box, which will unleash all sorts of problems including divisiveness, conflict and even foreign intervention. There is also an apprehension that federalism will add another layer of government complicating the woes of governance in the country. While these may be extreme views, it is true that federalism alone cannot solve Nepal's many-faceted problems of underdevelopment, social exclusion, and democratic deficit. Other political, economic and social instruments, such as decentralized local governance, inclusion, empowerment and representation, will still be required. Even after a federal structure is agreed upon, there will be demands for sub-regional nationalism, which has to be addressed variously including through creation of new states, devolution of power, decentralization, or better local governance system. From the experiment of federalism in India, where new states continue to be carved out of existing states, it has been seen that there is "no objective basis for determining the optimal size of states"[16] This question will continue to be raised as Nepal moves in the road towards federalism. Then, Nepal still needs to address the questions of inequality and exclusion which cannot be addressed through territoriality of federalism alone. There

---

[16] Khilnani et al. (2012), *op.cit.*

will still be unresolved issues of multi-layered government. The issues of women, smaller communities and geographically dispersed groups will remain unresolved either.

Lesson XII: Discourse on federalism should be transparent and inclusive. It should address the issues of identity and capacity as well as foreign policy and national security

The debate on federalism in Nepal will need more transparency in deliberation and in decision-making process. It has been evident in the past that esoteric backroom negotiation among top leaders of major political parties alone cannot dispel the apprehension of those who are afraid of losers and winners in the issue of federalism. It requires a wide participation of traditionally excluded groups, the Janajatis, Madhesis, and other fringe groups. For an informed discourse, there has to be wider discussion among the civil society and academic community. In particular, there should be more vigorous debate about suitable federalism in context of foreign affairs and national security, especially in relation to Nepal's geopolitical ground realities. For example, the high-level committee that the Constituent Assembly had appointed was not academic enough, as its members toed the party lines while recommending models of federalism, one of the sources of the current problem. Passion on identity alone will not solve the debate on federalism. The issue of capacity and viability, including in the context of foreign affairs, will have to be inevitably handled. Everyone involved in this process must understand that there will be no quick fixes. Neither can we borrow a template or model from elsewhere, though we can learn from best practices suitable to us. Nepal must tread carefully on the issue of federalism to avoid mishaps on the road ahead. Nepal's neighbours and friends need to demonstrate flexibility, understanding, support and cooperation in this regard.

Federalism: Perspectives on a Nepali model

Shambhu Ram Simkhada

Federalism can be understood as a theory or advocacy of federal principles for dividing the powers between member units and common institutions[1] within a nation-state. In its conceptual-philosophical realm, a regime can be defined as federal if it meets some simple criteria.[2]

- There should be at least two orders (tiers) of government, central and regional (provincial-state-cantonal) and local (municipal).

- Each of these tiers are constitutionally defined and have some genuine autonomy with clearly defined and devolved powers and functions.

- There should be an arbiter of the constitution, the courts, in case of disputes between the centre and the lower units or among the constituent units.

Federations are of enormous variety, centralized, decentralized, parliamentary, and presidential, with many or few units. For the federation to be functional the following fundamentals must be clear in the federalism debate:

- Nature and names of the constituent units

- Numbers

- Constitutionally defined division of powers and functions

---

[1] Federalism (Stanford Encyclopedia of Philosophy) p.1

[2] George R. M. Anderson, *Federalism: An Introduction* Forum of Federations The Global Network on Federalism, translated by Kedar Bhattarai, (UNDP, Kathmandu, Nepal, 2007)

- Acceptance of diversity, minority rights and rule of law
- Fiscal arrangements and economic viability
- Nature of the State and its political institutions
- The legal regime

Table No 1: Positions of Political Parties on the main issues of Federalism in Nepal

Political Parties	Nature / Name	Number	Division of power	Diversity / Representation	Fiscal Arrang- ement	Govt Structure	Legal Regime
UCPN Maoist	Single identity	10-14	already agreed	Inclusive	Already agreed	Bicameral Presidential	Constitutional Court - 5 yrs
Nepali Congress	Multiple identity	7-13	State Restructuring	Inclusive		Parliamentary Democracy	Existing System with modification
CPN (UML)	Multiple identity	7-15	Natural Resources	Inclusive		Directly elected Prime minister	Existing System with modification
Madheshi Morcha	Regional	demand of 1, compro- mise on 2	5 Schedules	Multiple identity -Single (2) Province		?	?
CPN- Maoist	National identity	14?		Inclusive		Bicameral Presidential System	Constitutional Court

Applying these principles to the Nepali debate on federalism, as the table above shows, there is consensus amongst the main political actors on many of the elements. The only remaining issues are the nature, names and numbers of the constituent units. Here, the principal stumbling block is the understanding of ethnic identity in relations to national identity. The unified Maoist party insists on ethnic identity based provinces with mixed names of what they define as excluded and marginalized groups. To accommodate this, they propose a relatively larger number of federal units (10-14). The Nepali Congress and the Communist Party of Nepal (Unified Marxist-Leninist) (CPN UML) insist on names reflecting multiple identities and a relatively smaller number of units (6 and 7 going up to 13 and 15). Economic viability and North - South access are also important considerations. The Madhesi Morcha started with the demand of a single province for the whole of the Terai-Madhesh but is ready to compromise on two provinces. The Unified Communist Party of Nepal (Maoist) (CPN-M) wants nationalities based identity but also wants to strengthen the identity of the Nepali nation-state as a whole.

On the fundamental issue of division of power, there is already broad agreement on three tiers, national, provincial and local with different schedules of powers and functions. Provisions for special arrangements for minorities within them have also been made. In case of diversity management and representation, there is agreement on the need for inclusion although this becomes a bit complicated when it comes to the Terai-Madhesh with their insistence on one or two provinces only. On Fiscal arrangements, revenue collection and sharing there are already broad agreements. Not much discussion has taken place on the structure of the government at the provincial/local level. But consensus has been reached on the state being inclusive and democratic with directly elected President and a Prime Minister elected by the Parliament sharing power at the centre. On the legal regime too, there is agreement on setting up a Constitutional Court for five years with the Chief Justice of the Supreme Court chairing the bench. So, aside from the 3 Ns (nature, name and number) of the constituent units, there is agreement among the main political parties on almost all issues. Why then has the debate on federalism divided Nepali society so much? What can be a Nepali model of federalism for all political actors to agree and move the political process forward?

Genesis

The idea of federalism may have been mooted long ago[3]. But the themes of the People's Movement of 2006, the principal fountainhead of the *politics of consensus* that has brought Nepal to this point were inclusive democracy and restructuring of the state. The Madhesh Movement became the rallying point for the demand for federalism. Clause 6 of the agreement signed between the Government of Nepal and Madheshi People's Rights Forum on August 30, 2007 states "While restructuring the state, an arrangement of a federal governance system comprised of provinces (Pradesh) with autonomy shall be made by keeping sovereignty, national unity and indivisibility of Nepal intact.[4]

In highly charged political environments, the demand for federalism was a natural reaction to the traditional over centralization of political power and economic resources in Kathmandu. Like many other political slogans, federalism too initially came up as a panacea to all problems rather than a well thought out road map for a democratic, peaceful and prosperous nation-state building. The weight of the Madhesh Movement in the aftermath of the successful People's Movement carried the demand of federalism through. So, the Interim Constitution of Nepal 2063 (2007), as amended reads "Nepal is an independent, indivisible, sovereign, secular, inclusive federal democratic republic State".[5] But as an international expert on and advocate of federalism and experienced hand in Nepal's latest constitution making suggests "Nepal became committed to federalism without actually having a large consensus on what it means in practice".[6] Here in lie the challenges and dilemmas of the federalism discourse and presenting perspectives on a Nepali model.

---

[3] Ram Raja Prasad Sing and Gajendra Narayan Singh were pioneers of republic and federalism in Nepal

[4] "Agreements and Understandings on Peace Negotiation of Nepal", Government of Nepal, Ministry of Peace and Reconstruction, Singh durbar, (Kathmandu, Nepal, Second Edition, 2008)

[5] Interim Constitution of Nepal 2063 (2007) with amendments of April 13, 2007 and July 12, 2008

[6] See George R. M. Anderson, "Towards a Suitable Federal Framework for Nepal" in *Nepal: Design Options for the New Constitution*, ed. Bipin Adhikari, Nepal Constitution Foundation, Tribhuvan University, Faculty of Law and Supreme Court Bar Association, 2010

Federalism - the main cause of the demise of the CA

The Constituent Assembly (CA) represented the long held aspiration of the people of Nepal to be governed democratically under a constitution written by their own elected representatives. The CA, the centerpiece of the Maoist movement, after several extensions of its initial two years term, was dissolved on 28 May, 2012 without completing the constitution or political agreements on the constitutional, political and practical problems. There were myriad reasons for the demise of the CA but questions on federalization of the Nepali state were at the core. Why has the debate on federalism divided Nepali politics to the extent that it became the principal cause of the dissolution of the CA and increasing discord amongst the main political actors to the extent that some of them are forming separate Federalist alliance excluding some of the other main partners instrumental in driving the whole peace process and bringing the country this far? The question is serious and the present discourse on Federalism, the first, I believe, after the demise of the CA, timely and vital but complex and challenging.

The Intellectual Challenge

Creating a democratic, peaceful and prosperous society, country, nation, state has never been an easy task for political leadership and statesmen anywhere.[7] Physical terrain, ethno-cultural diversity and geo-strategic location make Nepal an intricate laboratory of state formation and nation building. Dynamics of time and technology have made this more complex now. Amidst growing demands of identity, needs of better livelihoods, diverse political parties' interests, Nepal's local realities, national priorities and changing regional/global complexities, restructuring of the state become intellectually demanding, politically complex and economically difficult.[8] The whole

---

[7] For a discussion on what differentiates politics from leadership and statesmanship or politicians from leaders and statesmen, see Simkhada, Shambhu Ram *Politics, Leadership and Statesmanship*, LEAD Nepal 2009 and Power, justice and statesmanship, *The Kathmandu Post*, December 18, 2007

[8] Modern state formation and nation building in the developing world is a post-colonial phenomenon compared to the Westphalian experience of the Western world. For a discussion on the challenges of the vertical and horizontal evolution of the state system see Simkhada, Shambhu Ram "Global Human Rights Agenda: Emerging Issues" in *Reinventing the United Nations*, Eds. Ajit M. Banerjee and Murari Raj Sharma, Prentice Hall, India 2007

exercise now hinges on how the process starting from the Five Steps Path[9] to the 12-Point Understanding between the erstwhile Seven Party Alliance (SPA)[10] and CPN-M leading to Comprehensive Peace Agreement (CPA) all the way to the election and dissolution of the CA and transition to the republic can be managed.

Meaningful conclusion of this course means completing the remaining aspects of the peace process, particularly integration of the Maoist Army Combatants, agreement on the constitution, its promulgation and fresh elections. This makes agreement amongst the major political actors on the nature, numbers and names of the provinces crucial. Moving forward is going to be challenging in many respects but the challenge to the Nepali intellect may be the most serious. In the foreword of the book *Common Wealth* by Jeffrey Sachs, Professor Emeritus Edward O. Wilson of Harvard University writes "we exist in a bizarre combination of stone age emotions, medieval beliefs, and god-like technology. That, in a nutshell, is how we have lurched into the early twenty-first century."[11] If this is what thinkers feel in societies we regard as advanced, from which we are influenced and inspired, one can imagine the societies suffering from what an Indian diplomat-scholar calls *tragedy of mimicry* are going through.

Globalization of Economics-Localization of Politics

While presented powerfully, expressions of concern that the way mankind is organizing itself politically and economically is leading to dangerous divergences are however not new.[12] Tremendous transformation in science

---

[9] The Five Steps Path was the Roadmap presented by the President of the Nepali Congress and Leader of the SPA leading the People's Movement for the Restoration of Peace and Democracy in Nepal which laid the groundwork for the 12-Point Understanding and other political developments that followed.

[10] It should have been Seven Party Coalition (SPC) from the start as there are significant differences between Alliance and Coalition and the SPC was a collection of disparate political parties with the Nepali Congress Democratic on the right to many left parties and regional party such as the Sadbhawana, formed on short term interests but without long term goals let alone shared values.

[11] Sachs, Jeffrey *Common Wealth Economics for a Crowded Planet* (Allen Lane Penguin Group, UK 2008)

[12] Among many others, the recent Report of the UN High Level Panel on UN Reform, for instance talks of the growing cultural abyss in the world

and technology has enhanced the potential of peaceful and positive transformations but also increased the risks of uneven developments or more serious conflict and chaos. Increasing globalization of economics characterized by increased flow of goods, services, capital and people but growing localization of politics along ethnic, cultural, religious, linguistic and regional lines with their impact on further fragmentations of some societies is complicating the understanding and management of politics, economics and society.[13] But new ideas to respond to the challenges of change are in short supply. The idea deficit profoundly affects the current transition in Nepal in general and the federalism discourse in particular. What is the driving force of federalism, politics or economics, identity or livelihoods? How will the demands of political power division affect the fragmentation of the already small Nepali market?

Unless we think better and act faster, societies like ours can suffer the *worst of both the worlds* with the vicious cycle of poverty and conflict perpetuating indefinitely. It also means that we cannot rely on conventional wisdom to explain the problems facing us today nor look elsewhere for answers. We have to delve deeper into the depths of our own wisdom[14] as well as fly high in our creative imagination based on our history and experiences. But we must be open to ideas from anywhere as long as they promote peaceful and positive transformation as well as help us comprehend our local necessities, national realities and global complexities as we live in an increasingly globalizing world with great opportunities but also serious risks.

---

[13] Scholars warned of the growing discord between geo-centric economics and ethno-centric politics in the 1970s. Today the world faces the contradiction between globalization of economics, localization of politics. Paul Kennedy's Preparing for the Twenty First Century, Samuel Huntington's Clash of Civilizations, Noam Chomsky's Failed States and Pawan K. Varma's The Great Indian Middle Class best highlight the contradictions of the dynamics of Time and Technology but the rigidity of the Human emotions. How to reconcile between these two trends, both important for human development? See Simkhada Shambhu Ram *Issues Before the SAARC Summit*, Bangladesh Institute of International and Strategic Studies, Volume 10, No. 4 (1989), Dhaka, Bangladesh.

[14] See Simkhada et al, *Causes of Internal Conflicts and Means to Resolve Them, Nepal a Case Study*, Occasional Paper 3/2004, PSIO, Graduate Institute of International Studies, Geneva August 2004. Noble Laureate Amartya Sen presents a fascinating case of the inter-relationship between the search for identity and perpetration of violence in his book *Identity and Violence The Illusion of Destiny*, (Penguin Books, London, 2006)

Multiple Undertaking

The current Nepali state restructuring exercise is influenced by significant complexities; a nation-state is much more than the physical territory, it is the intrinsic unity of the multitudes of the people bound together around some shared values and a sense of common destiny. The Nepali nation-state came into existence through a successful exercise in military conquest but the requisite state-formation and nation-building process faltered. So, we are now trying to address the problem of nation building through state restructuring and creating an appropriate form of governance for inclusive democracy. This is happening within a specific context of peace building exercises after the end of a long violent conflict. Thus the state restructuring and nation building work are interlinked with peace building and constitution making process simultaneously.

Dilemmas

Dilemmas at conceptual-philosophical and practical-behavioral levels make the current multiple undertaking highly complicated. The balance between local autonomy and central authority for self-rule within shared rule is a complex issue in nation building experiences historically everywhere in the world but more so in Nepal because of its diversity and location. Time and technology have added to the geo-political complexity. At the same time, the demands for federalizing the Nepali state must be seen with proper considerations of the pressures on the state system globally with vertical or upward evolution towards supra-national arrangements and downward devolution to sub-national units. Non-governmental and non-state actors too are gaining greater power and influence in relations to the state at the horizontal level.[15] In such a context, what is the logic of self-rule for a region or a community within a state which survives on foreign aid, citizens go hungry without food aid from outside and its intellectual and institutional capacities are dependent on and dictated by intrusive INGOs? How to balance the demands of identity with the needs of better livelihoods? The current state building, peace building and constitution making exercises to be meaningful and durable, must build into it arrangements to reconcile

---

[15] See Simkhada, Shambhu Ram "Global Human Rights Agenda…"…op.cit

the significant dilemmas arising out of the dichotomy in economic and political management of societies being experienced in the world, mostly the developing world.

Security

These challenges are further complicated by the notion of security, national and human, arguably the central responsibility of the state. Prosperous democracies are built on the foundations of individual liberty, leveraged with safety and prosperity of society but all subordinated to the demands of national security. In building a prosperous and democratic state, traditional nation-state system is built on the foundation of monopoly over the legitimate use of violence. How can one conceptualize a nation-state system where multiple non-state actors challenge the state with violence? Yet, as Aristotle wrote long ago "justice is the principle of order in society". Therefore, unjust use of force will not be legitimate and hence will be challenged. So, the state will not be able to monopolize violence without society being seen as just. But as beauty, justice also lies in the eyes of the beholder. With terrorism, the notion of security and use of violence needs to be looked at in a whole new approach.

Fear of Federalism

Amidst all the complexities and dilemmas, everyone invokes "the people" to justify their individual, ethnic, regional and party agenda. But what is being done may have little to do with the people who want to enjoy the fruits of their hard work in peace, security and dignity, came out in the millions for the promise of a sovereign, independent, democratic, peaceful and prosperous Nepal for all Nepalis on several occasions. Is such a Nepal in the making? The first step in this journey is a realization that the real conflict here today is about political culture; what comes first, personal, community/party/regional or national interest? And the choices are simple, between right and wrong, justice and injustice, peace and violence, selfish power grab and honesty, compromise and sacrifice more than ideology, class, caste, ethnicity, religion or region on which politics is focused.

Diversity of caste, ethnicity, language, region, religion, division of ideologies with communists against democrats, communists against communists, democrats against democrats, Maoists against Maoists, NC against NC, UML against UML, monarchists against republicans, Hindu against secular, unitary against federal state, tussle between the judiciary and the executive and confusion even in the security sector - what are they if not signs of the classic Hobbesian *war of all against all* scenario? Perplexing as it may seem, despite poverty, illiteracy, injustice and exploitation of the past and chaos and confusion of today, culture of co-existence and tradition of tolerance is keeping Nepal together. In fact the ethnic, linguistic, religious and regional diversities with extremism of ideologies, fundamentalism of religions, psyche of intolerance and tools of violence, add people's hunger/anger, multiply them with egos, ignorance, arrogance, greed for power and conflicts of interests, mix them with regional/global complexities and how long will it take for Nepal to tear itself apart?[16] Such a scenario is creating a new fear of federalism. This fear is bound to lend support to those who see federalism as an instrument of discord and division.

In this confusion, the genuine demands of dignity and rights, better recognition and livelihoods, the real national agenda of durable peace, new constitution, free and fair election, good governance and rapid economic transformation for the welfare of all Nepalese through better utilization of internal resources and foreign investment are getting lost. No political party or leader has shared its/his vision of where and how it/he wants to take Nepal collectively as a society-country-nation-state in the next five, ten or twenty years. Without an agreement on such a vision how could the CA agree on restructuring the state and promulgate the Constitution? If this confusion persists and federalism becomes the main cause for prolonging the current transition further making peoples livelihoods more difficult, it will affect their support to the federalism agenda?

Functional Federalism

Out of 192 member states of the United Nations 28 are federal states. Over 60 percent of the world's population, some of the highly prosperous democracies do not live under federalism. So, it is not the only route to

---

[16] See Simkhada, Shambhu Ram "Bringing Nepal's Politics Back on Track", *The New Spotlight*, Kathmandu

better recognition, stable democracy, durable peace, good governance, economic development and prosperity. But the Interim Constitution is a document of consensus amongst all the major political actors. It has already made Nepal a federal republic. So, disagreements over it as the main cause of prolonging the current transition and misrule pushing Nepal to the brink of failure also makes no sense. This means agreement on a functional model of federalism with manageable number of units with nature and names which enable us to strengthen peace and democracy, manage our diversity without disturbing the culture of tolerance and coexistence among Nepalese of diverse ethnicity, language, religion and region is the best way forward. This requires the discourse on federalism to focus on enhancing the access of the people to the services of the state, make politicians and officials more accountable rather than the current focus on creating multiple mini-Kathmandus. The following steps could create the environment for agreement among all the political actors:

- Institutionalization of what has been already agreed upon at the last CA

- Agreement on the three Ns as far as possible

- Transitional arrangements on issues that need more work

- Agreement on mechanism to continue work on those issues

- Finalization and promulgation of the Constitution and free and fair election by a national consensus government.

- Handover power to the new political dispensation with fresh mandate

Federalism: Slogan, Symbol and Substance

At times of great changes politics revolves around some slogans for or against some symbols and institutions. But as the dust settles politics must move on to its substance, the welfare of the people. That is why a great thinker once wrote happiness of the people is the end of the civil society, goal of the government (state).[17] Structures of the state and its institutions,

---

[17] John Adams, one of the fathers of the American Constitution wrote this then.

Presidents, Prime Ministers, Governors, Chief Ministers, political parties, bureaucracy and security agencies are all instruments created to promote the welfare of the people–their safety, security, promote freedom from fear and want and protect their dignity and rights. And in that respect with people dying unnecessarily, strikes and bandhs making movement within the country more difficult, scarcities and skyrocketing prices making even essentials outside the reach of people and the same political parties which brought the peace process to this point now going for each others' throats, Nepali politics is moving backwards. Happiness of the people in power is becoming the substance of Nepali politics and end of the state. Without change in this political culture can federal Nepal make a more democratic, peaceful and prosperous society country nation state? Rather than focusing on healing the wounds and wiping the tears of the victims of old injustices and recent violence[18] Nepal's politics is being pushed towards ethnic and regional conflicts. In discussions with the leaders of the main political parties recently the President is reported to have warned them of the risks of Nepal becoming Afghanistan.

Ultimately, politics is about values and leadership. Exercising state power by ignoring right and wrong, compromising with vital national interests makes society unjust, nation-state weak. When they see this happening people begin to lose faith in the system and those running it. Lack of "values consensus" increases violence paralyzing the state. Effective governance can smooth the twists and turns of transition arresting violence and crime, improving justice and order. But a dysfunctional state exacerbates political division, economic stagnation; social decay and national decline internally, create distrust with friends externally.

Political wisdom, Oriental or Western, conventional or modern recognizes power as the principal instrument of politics but justice as its end. Modern nation-states, federal or otherwise, must develop fair and reasonable systems of sharing political power and economic resources through devolution downwards with autonomy to regions, districts, municipalities, villages with guarantees of citizens' basic rights, evolve

---

[18] See Simkhada, Shambhu Ram *Highways of Hope and Healing, the Kathmandu Post* 04-10-2008 and Politics of Healing and Hope, 05-01-2008

upwards to regional and global levels in order to benefit from globalization and horizontally share power with non-state actors. Any society, country, nation - state wasting time and resources threatening each other in the name of politics, economics, religion, language or region is unlikely to get out of the poverty trap or its people collectively get ahead of others.[19] How do societies that have not yet achieved minimum values consensus or developed standards, norms and practices nationally internalize and benefit from universal values or follow international standards, norms and practices? Societies in transition – tradition to modernity, feudalism to democracy may suffer more from the poverty of intellect unable to differentiate slogan and symbol from substance of politics, further aggravating the problems of exclusion and marginalization and making inclusive democracy and restructuring of the state difficult.[20]

Conclusion

Creating appropriate state structures for equitable sharing of political power and economic privilege is never easy. But the future can no longer remain the mirror image of the past. The Nepali state must be restructured to accommodate the demands of better recognition of identity and the needs of better livelihoods of all Nepalis. To avoid stagnation society must be based on merit and competition but at the same time creating a level playing field by enabling and empowering the traditionally excluded and marginalized to compete. Federalism can be one of the ways of responding to the need of restructuring the Nepali nation-state as an inclusive and prosperous democracy. But nation building demands statesmen capable of comprehending the needs and aspirations of the people, able to create structures and institutions, bring together committed and competent team of intellectuals and professionals to translate slogan into substance, dreams into realities. Only then the dream of democracy, peace and prosperity for all Nepalis can be a reality. The challenge is to move towards such a society by channeling the creative energy of all, the hungry and the angry, excluded

---

[19] Simkhada, Shambhu R. Poverty and Violence in South Asia, *Financial Times*, Karachi 26 Feb, 2005

[20] Simkhada, Shambhu Ram, Intellectual Traffic Jam, *The Kathmandu Post* 18 Feb, 2005

and the marginalized without discouraging the enlightened contribution of those who have benefited before and spontaneous participation of those who have made good use of the opportunities in the past.

Right to Self determination-Concepts and Limitations

Lalit Bahadur Basnet

The concept of the right to self-determination has been used and mis-used in Nepal without proper understanding of the meaning, historical context, relation with international law and its universal aspects. This paper delves into each of these critical features so as to bring about a holistic and comprehensive understanding of the terminology as well as its application.

The fundamental concepts of right to self determination are:-

- The right of the people to determine their own destiny.

- The right to allow people to choose their own political status and determine their own form of economic, culture and social development - free from outside interference.

- The free choice of people to determine their status.

Historical Context

John Locke (1960) and John Stuart Mill (1859) had propounded the concept of self- determination in the context of the 18th century as to address series of freedom struggles against the colonization in Western Europe. In the 20th century, U.S. President Woodrow Wilson propounded this concept as a guiding principle for reconstruction in Europe in the aftermath of World War I. He stated that "every people have a right to choose the sovereignty under which they shall live."

Legal basis of the Right of Self-Determination in International Law

This concept of the right to self determination entered international law through its formal inclusion in the United Nations Charter. Article 1(2) states, "the purpose of United Nations is to develop friendly relations among nations based on the respect of the principle of equal rights and self determination of peoples ......" Other international conventions such as International Covenant on Civil and Political Rights (ICCPR) and International Covenant on Economic, Social and Cultural Rights (ICSECR) have also mentioned this right under various Articles. The UN has further elaborated and reinforced its agreement of this principle by other declarations and general assembly resolutions.[1] An important and often cited paragraph of the world body states:-

> "With a view to the creation of conditions of stability and well-being which are necessary for peaceful and friendly relations among nations based on respect for the principle of equal rights and self-determination of peoples, the United Nations shall promote:
>
> A. Higher standards of living, full employment, and conditions of economic and social progress and development;
>
> B. Solutions of international economic, social, health, and related problems; and international cultural and educational cooperation; and
>
> C. Universal respect for and observance of, human rights and fundamental freedoms for all without distinction as to race, sex, language, or religion.

---

[1] The 1960 Declaration was followed by the 1970 General Assembly *Declaration on Principles of International Law Concerning Friendly Relations and Co-operation among States in Accordance with the Charter of the United Nations* (GA Res 2625 (XXV), 24 October 1970) further elaborated the principle of right to self-determination. Article 55 of the Charter also reinforces the importance of the right to self-determination:

Another declaration[2] also recognized,

"the need for the creation of conditions of stability and well-being and peaceful and friendly relations based on respect for the principles of equal rights and self-determination of all peoples, and of universal respect for, and observance of, human rights and fundamental freedoms for all without distinction as to race, sex, language or religion".

Likewise, Principle 5 of the1970 Declaration[3] states:

"By virtue of the principle of equal rights and self-determination of peoples enshrined in the Charter of the United Nations, all peoples have the right freely to determine, without external interference, their political status and to pursue their economic, social and cultural development, and every State has the duty to respect this right in accordance with the provisions of the Charter".

But one aspect needs careful attention. Who are the 'peoples' as mentioned in these various statements and resolutions that are entitled for self-determination? There is no definition in international documents about the right to self-determination that is to be exercised or a clear definitional direction of who the word 'peoples' refers to. However, academics have referred 'peoples' as inhabitants of nations and/or groups that share a sense of a group, solidarity based on language, lineage, ethnicity, culture and/or religion and a sense of political community rooted in their group identity.

The most common example of exercising this right in recent years has got to do with indigenous peoples within a State or sizeable (majority) ethnic groups not sharing a sense of commonality within the country. There are

---

[2] The 1960 *General Assembly Declaration on the Granting of Independence to Colonial Countries and Peoples*,(GA Res 1514 (XV), 14 Dec 1960)

[3] The 1960 Declaration was followed by the 1970 General Assembly *Declaration on Principles of International Law Concerning Friendly Relations and Co-operation among States in Accordance with the Charter of the United Nations* (GA Res 2625 (XXV), 24 October 1970) further elaborated the principle of right to self-determination.

also sufficient illustrations wherein certain minority groups have been regarded as 'peoples' though the level of rights enjoyed might vary (see the reference to application of an external right of self-determination below).

As a pre-requisite to Human rights

The UN, through various instruments, holds that the right of self determination is a pre requisite to the enjoyment of all other fundamental rights. In Vienna, in 1993, the United Nations world conference on Human rights affirmed that the right to self determination is part of the international law of human rights.[4] The Common Article 1 states:

- All peoples have the right of self-determination. By virtue of that right they freely determine their political status and freely pursue their economic, social and cultural development.

- All peoples may, for their own ends, freely dispose of their natural wealth and resources without prejudice to any obligations arising out of international economic co-operation, based upon the principle of mutual benefit and international law. In no case may a people be deprived of its own means of subsistence.

- Most recently, within the context of the Declaration of the Rights of Indigenous Peoples, there are several references to the right of indigenous peoples to self-determination:

    i. Article 3: Indigenous peoples have the right to self determination. By virtue of that right they freely determine their political status and freely pursue their economic, social and cultural development.

    ii. Article 4: Indigenous peoples, in exercising their right to self-determination, have the right to autonomy or self-government in matters relating to their internal and local affairs, as well as ways and means for financing their autonomous functions.

---

[4] Although not mentioned in the UDHR, the right of self-determination was recognised as a fundamental human right within the ICCPR and ICESCR

Secession vs integrity

Basically the right to self-determination is most frequently focused on two aspects:

(A) Internal Self-Determination

(B) External Self-Determination

The ambit of this phrase "the right to self determination?" contains two concepts: - As an internal issue, it permits free use of such state powers within the territory of the state. It does not mean partition of state sovereignty. In particular, political self-determination is autonomy within a State and participation in the State's political decision making process. As evident in the articulations in the ICCPR and ICESCR, there is a clear economic/financial aspect in terms of the 'right of all peoples to enjoy and utilize fully and freely their natural wealth and resources.' As in External Self-determination has been used in the context of decolonisation. The right of self-determination of peoples to decide whether to be independent, to remain a dependency or to merge with another State (free association or integration with an independent State) can be traced in the historical context of the British colonies gaining independence.

Some claim that it can be adopted to be a successor of any given state and allows the right to secession. Darrel Moellendorf says, "the most extreme form of self determination is secession". One can address the right of self -determination from a number of different perspectives. Claims of self determination led in part to the destruction of former Yugoslavia, and the spectre of secessionist movements has magnified the attention given to the rights of minorities and indigenous peoples. Today this concept has been claimed by the peoples of Baltic states of Estonia, Latvia and Lithuania, by other Nations under the Soviet Union, by peoples of the former Yugoslavia and by Eritrea, Slovakia and Quebec. The Jewish demanding this right to establish Israel, etc.

Allen Buchanan who is an expert in international law says that there can be a right to secede only if (a) the state grants a right to secede (as with the secession of Norway from Sweden in 1905), or if (b) the constitution of the state includes a right to secede (as does the 1993 Ethiopian constitution). The constitution of former USSR had provided right freely to secede from USSR but this provision was never used. This is a big and challenging question in international law. This principle obviously draws attentions to a basic contradiction between deferent norms and standard of international law. Sovereignty, territorial integrity and independence of states are fundamental concerns of international law and a coherent maintaining of such issues without pick and choose of where to and where not to apply are major tasks of international law. Latest issue is the case of Quebec of Canada. The Supreme Court of Canada declared that the Quebec legislature did not have a legal right under the constitution of Canada or under the international law to unilaterally secede from the country. However, the court also emphasized that the rest of Canada would have a political obligation to negotiate Quebec separation if a clear majority of provincial population voted in favour of it. At that time, the court stressed that in international law, self determination for peoples of groups within an independent state is achieved by participation in the political system of the state, on the basis of respect for its territorial integrity.

Therefore, contentious issue is whether there is a right of external self-determination beyond the context of decolonisation. In particular, whether the right of self-determination gives rise to a peoples' right to secede and form their own State.

- There is no consensus on this point. Most commentators stress that self-determination remains primarily a right having internal implications.

- The Supreme Court of Canada (regarding Secession of Quebec) in 1998 concluded: 'The recognized sources of international law establish that the right to self-determination of a people is normally fulfilled through internal self-determination – a people's pursuit of its political, economic, social and cultural development within the framework of an existing state. A right to external self-determination (which in this case potentially takes the form of the assertion of a right to unilateral secession) arises only in the most extreme of cases, and even then, under carefully defined circumstances'.

- The right of secession can arise only: where "a people" is governed as part of a colonial empire; [or] where "a people" is denied exercise of their political right or any meaningful exercise of their right to self-determination within the state of which it forms a part.

- The Court interpreted that the peoples of Quebec do not reach the point of secede as "threshold of the most extreme cases" since they had access to government, were equitably represented in legislative, executive and judicial institutions, occupied prominent positions within the government, freely make political choices and pursue economic, social and cultural development.

The demand of right to self determination in Nepal

Nepal is a multi- ethnic, multi lingual, multi-religious and multi cultural country. The right to self determination and caste/ ethnicity based federal system has become a great issue of discussion in political arena. Unified Communist Party of Nepal (Maoist) (UCPN (Maoist) party) and Madhesi alliance agreed to assure right to self determination with a right to secession. Likewise the indigenous and nationalities had been demanding federal autonomy with right to self determination. Maoist top leaders have also defined it as a right of secession. Maoist leader Suresh Alemagar says, "right to self-determination is more or less the right to secession; this is also the opinion of our political party". Likewise Prime Minister Dr. Baburam Bhattrai had said, "We will support the demands of peoples of Indian Kashmir, Assam and Northeastern states of India and Tibet also about the right to self-determination. What kind of determination is up to them to decide. We will support these kinds of demands raised in any part of the world including in America and Latin America and Africa. This is our ideology. Every one should be clear about our policy.[5]

But the Constituent Assembly which was dissolved in May 2012 in a report mentioned[6]

---

[5] Spotlight /April 25, 2008

[6] concept paper and preliminary draft report of CA, committee for restructuring of the state and distribution of powers, 2010, pp xix and 57

(1) Tribal people, indigenous nationalities, madhesi shall have the right of self-determination internally and locally in the form of politics, culture, religion, language, education, information, communication, health, settlement, employment, social security, financial activities, commerce, land, mobilization of means and resources and environment. These will be fixed later by making laws.

(2) There shall however not be any impingement on sovereignty, freedom, unity and regional integrity while enjoying the rights of self determination.

Perils and Possibilities of Nepal's Advent as a Federal State from the Perspective of Water Resources

Ratna Sansar Shrestha

Nepal as a Federal State

A debate has been raging about federalism in Nepal, with the declaration of Nepal as a federal state by the Interim Legislature-Parliament[1] in March 2007, by amending Article 138(1) of Interim Constitution of Nepal, 2007. Some oppose it dreading repetition of Yugoslavian history (which has disappeared from the world map following internecine ethnic conflict) and opine that Nepal should also learn lessons from Rwanda, Ethiopia, Sudan, etc. where ethnic conflict decimated the people.

The unelected Interim Legislature-Parliament has thus effectively preempted the Constituent Assembly (CA) in this respect, thereby violating the right of sovereign people to decide whether federalism is appropriate for Nepal or not and also to decide the manner of state restructuring, if majority of people in Nepal are in favor of federalism.

Majority of the members of the Committee on State Restructuring of the Constituent Assembly's recommended 14 provinces, of which about 10

---

[1] The reinstated House of REpresentative was renamed "Interim Legislature-Parliament" after inductiin 83 representatives of CPNM (eventually named UCPNM) in 2007 (equal to the presence of UML). Basically this wasn't a parliament comprising of popularly elected people's representatives.

were on the basis of single identities of certain ethnic groups[2]; minority opinion was separately submitted recommending 6 provinces, triggering a controversy. Later a High Level State Restructuring Advisory Commission was also constituted, under Article 138(2), which recommended 10 provinces mostly on the basis of single identities while those dissenting to it recommended 6 provinces without any reference to any identity.

As 118 ethnocentric groups have been identified so far in Nepal, formation of provinces based on identities of 10 ethnocentric groups will deprive the remaining groups from the right to recognition of their identities. Strangely, the proponents of identity based federalism prefer one contiguous province for the whole southern plain known as Terai, depriving several prominent ethnocentric groups in the area from recognition of their identities. This indicates lack of consistency and rationale in the approach and proposal to create provinces on the basis of identities.

Further, the federalists also have demanded right to self determination and autonomy to the provinces. Nepal is smaller than an average province of India and use of right to self determination and autonomy by the tiny provinces could entail in spinning off of tiny "sovereign" states that could cause headache even for India and China. On the other hand this will also mean that the ethnocentric groups that aren't fortunate enough to have separate provinces named after their groups will be deprived of the right to self determination and autonomy.

Furthermore, the proponents of identity based federalism are seeking preemptive rights to the ethnocentric groups in the provinces named after them. For example Newars in Newa Rajya will be entitled to preemptive right in every walk of life as well as in governance. This will render other ethnocentric groups in each of such provinces second class citizen. Similarly, it will also result in minority rule over majority as in all 10 proposed ethnocentric provinces, the main group is in minority (Newars are in minority

---

[2] These are not actually ethnic groups, rather ethnocentric groups with distinct ethnicity, culture, religion and language. For example there is no ethnic group called Newa. News people comprise of different ethnicity, religion and culture. Only language is common which is spoken in a number of dialects. Hence, it is referred to as ethnocentric groups throughout this paper, instead of ethnic group.

in the proposed Newa Rajya). Similarly, right to self determination and autonomy will also be exercised by the minority. These make the concept abhorrent to the most.

All of these pose a serious peril of flare up of ethnocentric conflict, as about 10 ethnocentric groups will become privileged class (by having their identities recognized and being conferred with preemptive right) while disenfranchising the remaining. What needs to be remembered is that what is being proposed isn't simple geographic division like districts, zones, development regions, counties, etc.

This has potential for the development of centrifugal tendency in as much as remaining 108 ethnocentric communities too will start demanding creation of separate provinces in recognition of their identities; perhaps in the line of demand for creation of "Telangana" state by carving up Andhra Pradesh in India for which agitation is ensuing. During his recent "home stay" with Chepang community, care taker PM Bhattarai promised a province even to Chepangs (population 52,237 scattered over 6 districts of Makwanpur, Chitwan, Gorkha, Dhading, Lamjung and Tanahu[3]) and at this rate other ethnocentric groups too will start demanding provinces based on of their respective identities.

Experts are of the opinion that the Interim Legislature-Parliament decided about it as if it enjoyed powers similar to that of an elected Constituent Assembly. This violates the right of the sovereign people to take decision in this respect after holding extensive brainstorming discussions and debates, subsequent to them being educated about manifestations and ramifications of federalism and also about the ramifications of the preemptive rights to be bestowed to about 10 ethnocentric groups. The decision process has deprived sovereign people from exercising their right to full and meaningful participation in decision through popularly elected body like Constituent Assembly (CA), which was effectively preempted by Interim Legislature-Parliament. An unelected body has no such right.

---

[3] 2001 Nepal Census.

This has polarized politicos, intelligentsia and the general public and has potential to open floodgate of ethnocentric conflict. Under the universally accepted principle of right to natural resources each Nepali citizen bred and brought up in any part of the country is entitled to equal right to the available natural resources of the country in any part of the country. For example, the Nepali people living in the concrete jungle of Kathmandu valley are entitled to the same equitably on the trees, plants, woods, wildlife, herbs, etc. of the forest in Terai. However, after the country is divided into different provinces under the federal system, complexities over sharing of natural resources is certain to arise. People of Manang district have misinterpreted the right to harvest 'Yarsagumba' (a medicinal herb) in their neighbourhood as their exclusive right and murdered 7 people from Gorkha in 2009 hunting for this herb in Manang. It has revealed that with the imminent implementation of federal structure people have started subscribing to the idea that people of one province will not get anything from the other province, even before the adoption of federalism in the country. Therefore, it is high time to analyze the negative impacts that may result while sharing water resources after the adoption of federalism.

One needs to treat the matter with the sensitivity it deserves as those discriminated against tend to migrate (emigration has already started from Terai, thereby devastating the local economy of Terai). In this modern age there are many ethnocentrically mixed couples and these will be torn apart during such migration. The offspring of such couples will suffer the most. One needs to learn lessons from the horrors of Indo-Pak partition.

People are advocating federalism as an antidote to unitary state, ignoring that each province will still be unitary. Besides, federalism has been proposed to alleviate problems of the downtrodden, marginalized, excluded, deprived, etc. But merely creating provinces in specific numbers will not solve these problems.

The silver lining will be in creation of employment in the form of opening of job opportunities as chief ministers, ministers, assembly members, commissioners, provincial judges, etc. in big numbers in the provinces. But this will create more problems (in terms of sustainability) than solve existing ones. It is estimated to cost an average of about Rs 500 million per province per year in the salaries and perquisites of such officials which totals Rs 7 billion a year that a country like Nepal could ill-afford (with Rs 7 billion, 700 km road could be built or 70 MW power project). Additionally, more funds will have to be invested in creating 14 provincial capitals.

Perils from the perspective of water resources

In Nepal's context, water resources, including other natural resources are as important as other issues like nationality, national integrity & security, ethnocentric identity, economy, etc. It will be better to be clear about the challenges of optimum exploitation of water resources, its management and usage of the benefit, including sharing thereof, for the betterment of Nepal and Nepali people in the federal context. It would have been better if the Constituent Assembly (CA) had discussed about optimum exploitation and the utilization of water resources in the interest of the country and formulated necessary provisions by arriving at a proper decision while adopting federalism in the country. If the country adopts federalism, the problems inherent to challenges pertaining to the utilization of water resources and sharing of benefit thereof needs to be addressed first. Water resource alone has potential to metamorphose Nepal from a backward, medieval economy to one comparable to India and China or forging ahead of them. Unfortunately, people have been discussing sharing/division of water resources subsequent to creation of provinces which will amount to division of flood and drought as Nepal is rich in flood during 4 months of wet season and drought in remaining 8 months. Nepal and Bangladesh, with the per capita water availability of 9,122 m^3 and 8,809 m^3 respectively, are deemed richer, compared to the neighbours (2,961 m^3 in Pakistan, 2,642 m^3 in Sri Lanka, 2,259 m^3 in China and 1,880 m^3 in India) but the ground reality is different. Paradoxical situation of "water, water everywhere but not a drop to drink" exists. This is mainly due to, especially in Nepal, flood during 4 months and drought in 8 months. Preferably, people should be aiming to share benefit after ensuring optimum exploitation of the water resources.

While some people and most political parties see only electricity in water resources. Others are able to see benefits that can be extracted from the multidimensional uses of water: adequate pure/clean water for consumption and sanitation (elimination of disease/death related to water and sanitation where many people die every year due to water borne disease), multiple cropping through irrigation to achieve food security (abolition of famine) including from animal husbandries and fisheries (cost effective nutritious food), navigation (water transport, fuel cost of which is more than 5 times lower than that of road transport), tourism based on water sports, its use for industrial purposes and even generation of substantial revenue from export of pure mineral water; besides electricity generation. What needs to be remembered is that there are alternative sources for electricity/energy but water has no alternative.

Despite being one of the natural resources, the nature and forms of utilization and benefiting thereof in the case of water resources is entirely different from other natural resources. It is necessary to identify the existing differences between water resources and other natural resources in the context of the federalism. By involving themselves and working as entrepreneurs local people can benefit directly from natural resources like land, forests, herbs, wildlife, minerals, etc. through extraction, collection, utilization and other forms of use, i.e. picking fruit from trees, cultivating land, collecting herbs, etc. Water resources, however, cannot be utilized and benefitted from in this manner. At the local level, people can benefit from micro irrigation schemes, micro hydropower, tourism based on water sports and other industries.

For example, cities use up most of the electricity which is mostly generated in hilly rural areas and these areas do not consume much electricity. Benefit from water resources can only be maximized by ensuring its optimum exploitation which is likely to be hindered by fragmentation of the country in very small units in the name of federalism. People are already discussing sharing/division of water resources under federalism which is futile without ensuring its optimum exploitation. Further, investment friendly environment will cease to exist due to interprovincial differences/conflicts when project site is in one province and upstream areas and downstream areas are in other provinces.

In deciding to implement federalism it should be ensured that there are no obstacles in the optimum exploitation of water resources, its management and usage of the benefit for the betterment of Nepal and Nepali people (if possible even downstream riparian countries like India and Bangladesh). Thus, it would be appropriate to hold discussions on the following points with regard to the water resources in federal state.

Drinking Water

We have age old practice of buying water source of one village by another village. After twenty years of conception of the idea of diverting water from Melamchi River of Sindhupalchowk district through underground tunnels into Kathmandu Valley to resolve the drinking water problem of the capital city, the work has started only recently. Although, this will deprive the local people from using the water of this river, traditionally used by them, no arrangement has been made to recompense them for the deprivation. In the meantime, local people have already put forward various demands for compensation, including sustained source of income for them. However, no arrangements have been made to meet their demand as it cannot be done by hiking the "price" of drinking water to incorporate "levy" expected by the people to whom the water "belongs" (the concept has been further complicated by ILO convention 169). If the intake area of this project is to be declared a separate province with right to self determination and autonomy and Kathmandu valley is made another province, the complexity of this project will get compounded.

What should not be forgotten in this respect is the heartrending incident of about 500 people's untimely death in 2008 due to the outbreak of diarrhea and cholera in several districts of Far Western and Mid Western development regions (Rukum and Jajarkot districts were the prominent ones) due to lack of potable drinking water and sanitation facilities. Besides, people are already getting killed due to dispute over water in several countries.

Multipurpose Project with Reservoir

A hydropower project with reservoir results in **magnitudinal** negative externalities than a run of the river project. The Kali-Gandaki hydropower project, which stores water on a daily basis, impacts less adversely than

Kulekhani hydropower project, which stores water around the year. Three negative externalities of a reservoir project are inundation/submergence (of land, forests and wildlife, tourist site, temple and infrastructure) and involuntary displacement and restriction on usage of water in the upstream areas.

While the people living in the upstream areas will be deprived from the consumptive uses of water (like, futuristic sounding, hydrogen economy) in order to ensure specific quantum of water for the reservoir as the project's electricity production will decrease if the quantum of water available is reduced, and consequently, project's revenue too will decrease; thereby rendering the project unfeasible. In order to avoid this, the Rule 10 of the *Electricity Regulation* guarantees specific quantum of the water to the licensee in accordance with the license. If the Upper Karnali Project, for example, is implemented, the people in Jumla will be denied the opportunity to consumptive uses of water from *Tila* River.

A reservoir project also results in positive externalities in the form of downstream benefits due to augmented/regulated flow and flood control. Augmented/regulated flow during the dry seasons will make multiple cropping possible through irrigation in the downstream riparian areas. Such water can also be used for drinking and sanitation, fishery and animal husbandry, water based industry, etc. The downstream areas will also benefit from water sport based tourism, navigation as well due to watershed improvement. Moreover, flood control means saving of life and limb from the ravages of flood and from subsequent saving of expenditure in repair and rehabilitation.

If a water resource project involves two or more provinces, while people in downstream province will benefit as water will become available during dry season for the purposes of irrigation, etc., but the province where the project is located will suffer due to inundation/submergence and involuntary displacement. And people in upstream province will suffer due to restriction on consumptive uses of water. In such a circumstance, the province where the project is to be located and the people in the upstream province will hardly be willing to have the project implemented. This has amply been demonstrated by Narmada, Kaveri disputes in India and dispute between Sindh and Punjab provinces about Kalabagh project in Pakistan.

In this backdrop, it will also be unfortunate if separate province/s is/ are created for the southern plains (Terai). Because, there is plenty of agricultural land but is dependent on monsoon rains for farming (no water); only one crop a year. It is not possible to avail adequate water in the dry season by building projects there in order to increase cropping intensity. Similarly, most of the industries are located in this region, but generation of electricity in cost effective manner is not possible in Terai. In other words, hills and plains are interdependent and complementarities exist. Actually, hills can become self reliant by building water resource projects, but same isn't possible in the plains (as no significant head and storage space is available). Therefore, Terai will suffer more after becoming separate province/s.

Mid-hills provide ideal location for building multipurpose project based on water resources that will result in involuntary displacement which requires resettlement. The paradox is: construction of a hydropower project with reservoir is not possible in the plains and there is not enough land in the hilly area to resettle people displaced by such a project. Conversely, there is plenty of land for resettlement in Terai but if Terai is declared a separate province, resettlement of people from hills will be unacceptable. Tharus of the Western Terai have already refused to resettle the people to be displaced by the West Seti Project.

Hydropower

From the perspective of production and use, even though the Western development region produces the highest quantum of electricity (about 330 MW) in the country, it consumes less than half of what it produces. However, the Eastern development region consumes 20 times more electricity than what it produces (14 MW). The Central development region consumes a little more than it produces (275 MW). Even if the existing five development regions are to be declared as five provinces, this type of happy sharing will not be possible. Simple issue like pricing can spin out of control and provinces with more generation capacity can shut off power if the price is not right. There is even a possibility that if India offers higher rate, then a province could choose to export rather than supply to other provinces.

Delineation of boundaries

Rivers have been used to delineate most of the districts, zones and development regions of Nepal since long time. In various permutations of provincializaiton rivers have been used as boundaries. This will be unfortunate as two provinces may have different aspirations, needs and priorities, which will result in disputes forcing non-implementation of water resource projects.

Impact on other Ganga basin courtiers

Adverse impact of creating provinces in Nepal in such a way that upstream/downstream riparian areas and project sites lie in different provinces, putting impediments in optimum exploitation of Nepal's water resources, will spill over on Ganga basin countries like Bangladesh and India too. Because, as estimated by Water Environment Partnership in Asia (WEPA), approximately 70% of dry season flow and 40% of annual flow of the Ganga River comes through Nepal. Therefore, Nepal is strategically located to augment flow in dry season and control flood in wet season, twin positive externalities, which is not possible, efficaciously, in the plains of Bangladesh and India. Back of the envelop calculation, therefore, will show that around 40% of flood in Ganga basin countries can be controlled by building reservoir projects in Nepal.

The terrain and topography of Nepal affords opportunity to add temporal and spatial value in terms of flood control and provide augmented/regulated flow during dry season for irrigation; generating high value electricity (peak-in power) cost effectively as a byproduct. For the purpose, reservoir projects will have to be built in Nepal's mid-hills. Close cooperation between future provinces of Nepal, focusing on proper apportionment of both positive externalities and negative externalities, is *sine qua non.*

Similarly, John W Handmer has opined that "Kali Gandaki 1 and 2, Seti, Trisulganga, Sapta Koshi, etc. may prove more than adequate to meet all the reasonable water demands in Ganges basin covering Nepal, India and Bangladesh."[4] Further, in October 1986 a Joint Committee of Experts

---

[4] John W Handmer. "Discussion of *Risk Information for Floodplain Management*" by L. Douglas James and Brad Hall (October 1986, Vol. 112, No. 4)." *Journal of Water Resources Planning and Management.*, 114(1), 1988 , pp 120–122.

from India and Bangladesh had proposed 7 storages in Nepal to augment the dry season flows of the Ganga at Farakka[5]: Karnali/Chisapani, Kaligandaki 1, Kaligandaki 2, Trisulganga, Seti, Sapta Koshi and Pancheshwar. But this will not be possible with Nepal getting fragmented into several states resulting in upstream/downstream riparian areas and project sites falling in different provinces.

Specifically, it has been reported that water table is declining at a rate of one foot per year averaged over the Indian states of Rajasthan, Punjab and Haryana, including the national capital territory of Delhi, an area in North Western India that covers more than 438,000 square kilometers[6]. Augmented/regulated flow in dry season from Pancheshwar project can quench thirst of these areas.

Possibilities from the perspective of water resources

In the endeavor to explain possible perils, an attempt has already been made to explain the possibilities to metamorphose Nepal's economy in the context of federalism putting up impediments in its path. Therefore, no repetition is warranted. On the other hand, it has not been possible to attain optimum exploitation of Nepal's water resources under centralized unitary system. People are already debating about sharing and division of the water resources after provincialization. What needs to be remembered is that without ensuring optimum exploitation, what could be shared/divided in the situation obtaining at the moment is the sharing/division of flood during 4 months of rainy season and drought in 8 months of dry season. In the case of water resources, Nepal and her people can benefit only by ensuring optimum exploitation (ensuring no obstacles in the optimum exploitation of it), prudent management and sharing of the positive externalities from multidimensional uses of the water resources and bearing negative externalities equitably.

---

[5] Sapta Koshi high dam can help solve dispute between India and Bangladesh due to Farakka barrage.

[6] http://www.scientificamerican.com/article.cfm?id=is-india-running-out-of-water

Due to lack of river basin approach, sites that can result in multidimensional benefit have been "given" away as projects such that not only Nepal but even India will be deprived from benefits. A prominent example is Upper Karnali project, which is an ideal site for 4,180 MW installed capacity with reservoir that has potential to irrigate up to 1.5 million hectares of land in dry season and also control flood. As Nepal doesn't have land in that quantum in the downstream area of the project site the logical beneficiary of it would have been UP and Bihar in India. More importantly, according to Dr A.B. Thapa[7] "the Upper Karnali Storage Project would roughly be able to generate almost half of the electricity generated by the Karnali Chisapani Project (20,800 GWh) only at one third cost of the latter" (installed capacity 10,800 MW). However, Government of Nepal (GoN) has already issued a license for this project as a run-of-the-river project of 300 MW (in the name of optimization, its installed capacity has been raised to 900 MW, still as a run-of-the-river scheme).

In view of the above, the best solution for Nepal is to declare provinces on the basis of river basins of 3 main river systems as illustrated below:

MAP OF NEPAL
ADMINISTRATIVE DIVISION
75 Districts, 14 Zones, % Regions

Internal Boundry
Regional Boundry
Zonal Boundry
District Boundry

KTM - Kathmandu
B - Bhaktapur

©ncthakur.itqo.com

Sapta Koshi-Mechi
सप्तकोशी मेची राज्य

Sapta Gandaki
सप्त गण्डकी राज्य

Karnali-Mahakali
कर्णाली महाकाली राज्य

CHINA

INDIA

As Mechi River has a limited catchment area, we can have one Sapta Koshi-Mechi province in eastern Nepal. The river basin of Sapta Gandaki could be declared as the second province. Mahakali River too has a limited catchment area in Nepal, and therefore, we can have Karnali-Mahakali province in west Nepal. The right to decide the optimum level of exploitation of the rivers of a province should rest with the concerned province by adopting river basin approach.

However, a Federal Constitutional Commission on Natural Resources at the center will have to be created to, among others, monitor/regulate work of provinces with respect to water resources in order to ensure optimum exploitation, effective management and best use and sharing of the benefits. Besides, this commission can also settle disputes that may arise amongst provincial or local governments. Despite our long experience in social, cultural and religious diversity in the country, in view of the inevitability of our interdependence, lack of capacity, and inexperience of the federal system, maximum utilization of the country's water resources would be possible only if the residual power for its management rests with the Centre.

There is a already a provision in Interim Constitution for parliamentary ratification of, accession to, acceptance of or approval of treaties related to division/sharing of natural resources or of benefits thereof in Article 156. This provision will have to be enshrined in the new constitution for parliamentary ratification of/accession to/acceptance of/ approval of treaties related to division/sharing of natural resources or of benefits thereof amongst provinces of Nepal or between a province of Nepal and a neighbouring country in case a province with right to self determination is to be allowed to sign treaties with foreign countries.

Conclusion

CA has died its natural death due to expiry of its term without promulgating a constitution. Bhattarai cabinet has already been rendered care taker as PM Bhattarai on his ceasing to be a member of CA. Besides, the country has also lost its legislature; CA was also working as a legislature (had a constitution been promulgated, CA would have continued as a legislature till another is elected). Therefore, Nepal has now no government with executive authority, no legislature and not even a constitution (thankfully, the interim constitution is still in place and valid).

The care taker government is refusing to make way for a new government with executive authority unless consensus is reached regarding federalism and constitution. But the country is looking at a dead-end of one way street due to statements from the coalition in the care taker government that no constitution shall be acceptable without federalism and also that federalism, if it isn't based on recognition of single ethnocentric identity, will too won't be acceptable. On the other hand, identity based federalism will overshadow identities of over 100 groups and deprive them from right to self determination and autonomy availed to other groups.

Further, implementation of federalism in Nepal on these lines will create second class citizenry as well as result in rule of minority over majority. In view of this, it is unlikely that people will accept federalism on the basis of identities of a few ethnocentric groups. This has amply been demonstrated by several opinion polls conducted by several institutions over several years. Therefore, the best way forward is to conduct a referendum in which people will be asked whether Nepal should be a federal state and also whether provinces should be created on the basis of single identities or on, for example, water resources, if Nepal is deemed fit for federalism.

On the other hand, how the issue pans out is of utmost importance even to downstream riparian countries like India and Bangladesh; besides, most importantly, Nepal. Conversely, all three countries will end up losing if provinces are created as it will come in the way of optimum exploitation of Nepal's water resources; deprive from positive externalities like flood control and augmented/regulated flow in dry season.

Therefore, three provinces should be created on the basis of watershed of three major river systems (river basin approach) in order to maximize benefit from positive externalities from water resources, not only for Nepal but also for downstream riparians like India and Bangladesh; for example it can become possible to travel in a steamer from Benighat on Prithvi Highway in Nepal through to the sea port on Bay of Bengal near Dhaka of Bangladesh via India around the year if things are handled prudently.

Finally the problems of marginalized, excluded, downtrodden, deprived et al will not be solved by carving out (fragmenting) a small country like Nepal into over 10 provinces. Devolution of legislative authority to grassroots (municipal or village level) by enshrining it in the constitution will only solve the problem which is not a matter for delegation or decentralization. Because the center may choose to decentralize or delegate or not to do so, but authority vested in the grassroots by enshrining in the constitution will not depend on the vagaries of the leaders at the centre.

Engendering Human Rights in the federal Scheme: Reflections on Proposals for New Constitution

Raju Prasad Chapagain

Nepal has vowed to restructure the state into a federal system of government through adopting a new constitution that embraces universal values of democracy and human rights. The Interim Constitution of Nepal, 2007 (herein after "Interim Constitution") was amended in May 2008 to declare Nepal as a Federal Democratic Republic[1]. Subsequently, the Interim Constitution's Fifth Amendment strengthened the notion of federalism by directing the Constituent Assembly to create autonomous provinces that can enjoy full rights consistent with the aspirations of different communities in Nepal[2]. Accordingly, the Constituent Assembly worked towards drafting the new constitution but finally came to its dissolution due to failure of accomplishing its task within the given deadline[3]. This failure by and large resulted due to lack of consensus on federalism related issues.

---

[1] See, 4th Amendment of the Interim Constitution adopted on 28 May 2008. Article 4 of the Constitution reads."Nepal is an independent, indivisible, sovereign, secular, inclusive and federal democratic republican state."

[2] See, Article 138 (1A) of the Interim Constitution added by the 5th Amendment dated 12 July 2008. The added provision reads, "Accepting the aspirations of Madhesi people, indigenous ethnic groups and people of the backward and other regions for autonomous regions, Nepal shall be a Federal Democratic Republic. The provinces shall be autonomous with full rights. The Constituent Assembly shall determine the number, boundary, names and structures of the autonomous provinces and the distribution of powers and resources, while maintaining the sovereignty, unity and integrity of Nepal"

[3] The Constituent Assembly elected in May 2008 came to an end after its extended deadline elapsed on 28 May 2012.

There were so far some efforts in crafting the federal scheme of Nepal under the framework of New Constitution. Among them, the production of the Report of the CA Committee on the Restructuring of the State and Distribution of Powers (herein after called "State Restructuring Committee") and the report of the High Level Commission for Suggestions on State Restructuring (herein after called "State Restructuring Commission") formed as mandated by the Interim Constitution are notable. However, these efforts have not succeeded towards bridging divergence among wide ranging stakeholders including political parties in relation to a significant numbers of issues pertaining to federalism. These issues basically include the creation of the federal structures, right to self-determination, political preferential rights (*RajnaitikAgradhikar*) and local self-governance and autonomy. In addition, the role and responsibility of different levels of government for effective implementation of human rights provisions and how human rights provisions do apply across the future provinces have been overshadowed. It is noticeable that these issues directly relate to Nepal's binding obligations under wide ranging international human rights treaties from International Covenant on Civil and Political Rights (hereinafter called "ICCPR") to International Convention against Caste Discrimination (hereinafter called "ICERD") to ILO Convention 169 etc. It is therefore important for the political parties and other stakeholder to seek a resolution of these issues into line with the international legal standards enforceable on Nepal.[4]

With this backdrop, this paper is aimed at unravelling the gaps and weaknesses of the proposed constitutional provisions in light of Nepal's international human rights commitments through conducting an independent legal analysis and thereby promoting the human rights based resolution of the federal issues. Based on the outcome of analysis, the paper also offers a number of recommendations with a view to promote constructive dialogues and foster broad consensus among wide ranging stakeholders.

---

[4] Supreme Court of Nepal, in *Rina Bazracharya Case* (Writ No 2812 of 1998), highlighted the importance of the international human rights treaties by labeling them as "scriptures of Modern Era". The Interim Constitution, in its Article 33M, directs the state to effectively implement international treaties to which Nepal is a party.

Constitutional Objective of Federalism

At the outset, it is important to consider why Nepal chose to go for a federal system. Looking at the Comprehensive Peace Accord and the Interim Constitution 2007, it appears that the federalism was envisioned as a solution to long-standing social, economic and political problems of Nepal. Does federalism solve all the problems of a country? No. Experts in the field of constitution and federalism do not believe that federalism is a panacea to all the problems of a country[5]. However, knowingly or unknowingly, federalism has been portrayed as a solution to all the problems not only by the Interim Constitution but also draft provisions proposed by the Constituent Assembly Committee on State Restructuring and the High Level Commission on State Restructuring. According to them, the federalism would bring to an end to discrimination based on 'class, caste, language, sex, culture, religion and region'.

Federalism can obviously guarantee power to the regional and local units of the government through written constitution, a fundamental law of the land. Similarly, such constitutionally guaranteed distribution of power and self-government facilitate the process of creating conducive environment to bring about greater equality and fairness in society. It is also believed to promote enhanced access to and wider participation of people in the governance system at the different levels. But it is wrong to envisage that federalism can achieve simultaneously all the specified objectives. That is why the federalism related provisions incorporated in the preamble proposed for the new constitution should be revised to correspond to the reality. Otherwise, the federal system is likely to be source of frustrations among the common people once the aspirations of are remained unaddressed and that may ultimately lead to erosion of the legitimacy of the system itself.

---

[5] See, Interim Constitution, art. 138; 'Preamble' proposed by the State Restructuring Committee and State Restructuring Commission for new constitution.

Creation of State Structures

Provinces

The State Restructuring Committee proposes to create 14 provinces based on diverse grounds[6]; whereas, the State Restructuring Commission recommends for 10 geographical provinces and one non-geographical *Dalit* province[7]. There are also a number of dissentions from CA members with regard to number and name of the provinces proposed by the committee and the commission[8]. Given the facts, these issues remain highly contentious. Communities do also have opposing views, concerns and aspirations in terms of these issues. Especially, the demand for determining name of the provinces along line of mono-ethnic identity remains problematic. This has been stressed with a view to recognize the ethnic identity. The state should protect and promote different ethnic, religious, linguistic and any other identities. But naming of a province is not the only way to recognize the identities. If an identity of an ethnic group that has largest population in the respective province is taken as a sole basis for naming, other groups might feel that their identities have not been recognized and they have been excluded. It is also argued that the naming of the provinces along the line of ethnic identity may promote superiority complex for the ethnic group on which basis the province derived its name and others groups might feel inferiority complex. Such a case will not be helpful for effective functioning of the federal system. Looking at this issue in light of the right to equal protection and non-discrimination, it is desirable to take an approach that is secular in terms of ethnicity so as to make sure that all groups feel ownership toward the provinces. This is also in line with the recommendations of the Committee[9].

---

[6] See, Section 5(1) of the draft text proposed by the State Restructure Committee.

[7] See, Section 5 of the draft text proposed by the State Restructure Committee.

[8] See, State Restructuring Committee's Report, Page 180. One of the dissentions put forward by the CA members is to create seven provinces only.

[9] See, State Restructuring Committee's Report, Page 28, 29. In its report, the Committee stresses the importance of choosing the name of provinces that become acceptable for all.

Though the number of the provinces does not seem to have a direct link to human rights, how many provinces are created and how their borders are drawn may matter in terms of practical enjoyment of human rights. It is important to note that the root causes of the conflict and other social and political movements in Nepal directly relate to the denial of economic, social and cultural rights. In such a situation, if too many provinces are created and their borders are drawn without allowing such province to take proportional benefit from geographical and natural conditions, the economic capacity of the province to deliver may be slim and is likely to create barriers in enjoyment of economic and social rights. It is therefore important to keep the number of provinces reasonable and make sure that existing economic interdependence of the people from Himalayan, hilly and Terai regions be strengthened. If consensus is not reached in relation to these issues, a democratic and human rights friendly process should be agreed upon. For example, a commission was created in South Africa and referendums were held in Switzerland in order to accomplish these tasks. If sustainability of a federal system is desired, there is no alternative to ensuring 'reasonable accommodation of identities' that exist in society. One of the important factors for success and sustainability of a federal system relate to cherishing the values of federalism that include rule of law, compromise, consensus, cherishing of diversity, respect for minorities and tolerance. Otherwise, the federalism will not survive. If process of creating the structures goes against these values, it certainly fails to be sustained and succeed. If provinces and other structures are created along the line of mono-ethnic identity undermining the aspirations of other groups, there will be lesser chance to secure wider public acceptance and ownership over the federalism. Therefore, it is important to consider multiple identities as basis for creating the units so as to ensure legitimacy that enables all to feel stake in constitution's continued operation. There must also be a balance between effective centre for securing shared objective through joint actions and effective provincial government giving genuine self-rule at the regional level. Let's have a look at what, Yash Ghai, one of the renowned constitutional scholars, stresses the importance of creating the regional structures that embrace the full diversity of the region which will provide a basis for collective decisions and promote a sense of common purpose and in due course a common identity[10]. At the same time, he highlights the fact that no significant areas where there is a concentration of a linguistic or religious community that could form the basis of ethnic self-government.

Local Self-Government

Though it is *sin qua non* for securing socio-economic and political justice at grassroots level, the CA committee reports fail to ensure the local government as "institution of self-government". The Committee proposals have so far left for the province to arrange for local governments through making law. This seems against a broad-based consensus that local self-government should be guaranteed constitutionally. Local self-governance is myth not a reality unless the new constitution guarantees autonomy of local bodies in matters of resources, decision making, implementing decisions in assigned functions, and inviolability of its representativeness. It is important to notice the Indian experience in relation to local self-governance. Originally, the matter of local self-governance was left for the provinces, but subsequently the Indian Constitution was amended to institutionalize local self-governance.[11] There shouldn't be any hesitation in terms of guaranteeing the local government's autonomy in the new constitution as the guarantee of local self-governance is indispensable for creating a conducing environment for addressing long-standing socio-economic injustices in the country. The proposal to leave the local government issues at the discretion of the province is not fair. Merely entrusting the federal governments with the power to set certain standards[12] related to local governments doesn't protect the sanctity of the local self-governance.

---

[10] See, Intenational Journal of Minority and Group Rights,Martinus Nijhoff Publishers, Vol 18, No 3, 2011, P. 328, 329.

[11] See, 73rd and 74th Amendment (1992) to the Indian Constitution.

[12] The State Restructuring Committee and the State Restructuring Commission empower the center government to set certain standards in terms of formation of local governments.

Special Structures

In addition to creating the different level of state structures, the Committee on State Restructuring and the High Level Commission proposed to create special structures including autonomous regions, protected regions and special region[13]. In the drafts, the Committee and the Commission propose to create 22 special autonomous structures for a category of *Adibasi/ Janajati* groups[14]. For other groups which do not fall under the specified 22 groups, the State has been empowered to create a separate structure through making a law. The practice of adopting different measures with a view to address social discrimination and equality is usual. This is also encouraged under the international human rights law as a means to redress historical marginalization and exclusion. Such special structures are created in order to make such structures more autonomous than other structures. There is no doubt that there exist social and economic injustices which should be addressed through adopting a number of appropriate measures. There should be an imperative for the state to mainstream excluded and marginalized groups through protection and promotion of their language, culture and traditional knowledge, ensuring political participation and representation and access to land and natural resources and benefits generated through it. Looking at the proposals, the list of powers of special structure seems identical to the list of the powers designated for local governments. It appears that there is no clarity in the explanatory notes that how the creation of these structures with powers similar to the local government help the specified ethnic groups. There is also the question why only 22 ethnic groups and whether the beneficiary communities deserve to be consulted before going for a particular measure for the purpose of empowering such community[15]. Rather than creating the special structures in the constitution itself, it seems pragmatic for the New Constitution to pave the way for creating an autonomous geographical unit, in consultation with the communities, within the province for a group that is distinct (e.g. in terms

---

[13] See, common article 8 of the draft texts proposed by the State Restructuring Committee and the State Restructuring Commission.

[14] The classified ethnic groups include: Kochila, Jhangad, Dhimal, Meche, Santhal, Lepcha, Yakkha, Chepang, Dura, Kumal, Danuwar, Pahari, Majhi, Baram, Thamali, Chanthyal, Sunuwar, Danuwar, Surel, Jirel, Helmu and Bayasi.

[15] See, article 5 (c) and 6(a) of the ILO Convention 169. These provisions obligate the state to consult with the concerned groups.

of culture) and concentrated in a particular geography. For this purpose, a commission can be created to consult the communities, study their peculiar problems and suggest the geographical and non-geographical measures, within the permissible limit of the international human rights standards that are necessary to empower the marginalized ethnic groups.

Federalism Related Collective Rights

Self-determination

There have been proposals for guaranteeing a number of federalism specific rights including the right to self-determination. With regard to right to self-determination, both CA Committee on Restructuring and High Level Commission seem to have adopted an understanding that only internal dimension of self-determination is relevant in the given context of writing a new constitution.[16] This is in line with international law and jurisprudence.[17]

---

[16] See, article 12 (1)(2) of the draft text proposed by the State Restructuring Committee.

[17] See, General Recommendation no 21 adopted by the CERD Committee in 1996. The Committee elaborates on the external and internal dimensions of the right to self-determination: "In respect of the self-determination of peoples, two aspects have to be distinguished. The right to self-determination of peoples has an internal aspect, that is to say, the rights of all peoples to pursue freely their economic, social and cultural development without outside interference. In that respect there exists a link with the right of every citizen to take part in the conduct of public affairs at any level, as referred to in article 5 (c) of the International Convention on the Elimination of All Forms of Racial Discrimination. In consequence, Governments are to represent the whole population without distinction as to race, colour, descent or national or ethnic origin. The external aspect of self-determination implies that all peoples have the right to determine freely their political status and their place in the international community based upon the principle of equal rights and exemplified by the liberation of peoples from colonialism and by the prohibition to subject peoples to alien subjugation, domination and exploitation." (Para 4) "In the view of the Committee, international law has not recognized a general right of peoples unilaterally to declare secession from a State. In this respect, the Committee follows the views expressed in An Agenda for Peace (paras.17 and following), namely, that a fragmentation of States may be detrimental to the protection of human rights, as well as to the preservation of peace and security. This does not, however, exclude the possibility of arrangements reached by free agreements of all parties concerned." Similarly, see, article 4 (Indigenous peoples, in exercising their right to self-determination, have the right to autonomy or self-government in matters relating totheir internal and local affairs, as well as ways and means for financing their autonomous functions) and article 46 (Nothing in this Declaration may be interpreted as implying for any State, people, group or person any right to engage in any activity or to perform any act contrary to the Charter of the United Nations or construed as authorizing or encouraging any action which would dismember or impair, totally or in part, the territorial integrity or political unity of sovereign and independent States.) of the UN Declaration on Rights of the Indigenous People, 2008.

However, the languages proposed for the new constitution appears ambiguous and problematic in the sense that there lacks clarity on what legal claim can be made under the proposed provisions[18]. Merely a mention of "right to self-determination" doesn't ensure self-governed status of the excluded and marginalized groups on equal footing to the status of mainstream population. Rather, it may be achieved through effective implementation of federalism as a whole.

Instead, it is pragmatic for the new constitution to provide for measures including autonomy in matters related to their internal or local affairs, participation in State decision-making on equal footing on issues of cultural integrity and socio-economic development. It is advisable to consider the recommendations suggested by Prof. Anaya, Special Rapporteur on Rights of the Indigenous People in his report on Nepal 2009[19]:

> "Proposals for the design of a new federal structure should advance the self-determination of the Adivasi Janajati, which means advancing their exercise of the right to autonomy or self-government in relation to their own affairs, including the right to maintain their own customary laws and justice systems with due respect for universal human rights; the right to participate in decision-making at all levels of authority in relation to all matters affecting them; rights over territory and natural resources in accordance with customary patterns; and the right to maintain and develop the various aspects of their distinctive cultures. Federalism proposals should be developed with these and related rights in mind, in a spirit of flexibility and accommodation, without focusing on predetermined outcomes for the federal structure."

---

[18] See, article 12(1)(2) of the draft text proposed by the State Restructuring Committee and the State Restructuring Commission.

[19] See, Para 88 of the Report by the Special Rapporteur on the situation of human rights and fundamental freedoms of indigenous people, A/HRC/12/34/Add.3, 20 July 2009.

Preferential or Prior Rights

The draft texts of the Committee and the Commission contain proposals to reserve 'provincial chief executive position' (as proposed by the Committee) for a member of ethnic group that is largest in terms of population within the respective province and 'chief of special autonomous unit' (as proposed by the Commission) for two terms[20]. This has been put forward as a matter of political preferential right for historical marginalization of ethnic groups. Though the idea of compensating for historical marginalization/exclusion is embraced in international human rights law, the proposed provision exceeds the permissible limits as this provision bars other groups to compete for that position. Temporary measures are aimed to enable excluded groups to enjoy the right to equality at par with other mainstream groups. But such measures are not allowed to create an exception to general application of right to equality and non-discrimination[21]. It is therefore recommended to replace such provision with other affirmative measures into line with the international human rights standards[22].

Protection of Minorities

Nepal is already a country of minorities and more intra-provincial minorities will be created after state is restructured. Given the fact, adequate constitutional protection of minorities is indispensable. It is noticeable that there have been proposals for empowering the government, in general, to adopt positive measures for the development and protection of minority groups. However, the draft provisions proposed in the context of making

---

[20] See, article 13 of the draft text proposed by the both: State Restructuring Committee and the State Restructure Commission.

[21] Para 3 of the CERD Committee's General Recommendation 32 reads, "Special measures should be appropriate to the situation to be remedied, be legitimate, necessary in a democratic society, respect the principles of fairness and proportionality, and be temporary. The measures should be designed and implemented on the basis of need, grounded in a realistic appraisal of the current situation of the individuals and communities concerned."

[22] UN Human Rights Committee's General Comment 25 reads, "In contrast with other rights and freedoms recognized by the Covenant (which are ensured to all individuals within the territory and subject to the jurisdiction of the State), article 25 protects the rights of "every citizen". State reports should outline the legal provisions which define citizenship in the context of the rights protected by article 25. No distinctions are permitted between citizens in the enjoyment of these rights on the grounds of race, colour, sex, language,religion, political or other opinion, national or social origin, property, birth or other status."

new constitution do not ensure adequate provisions offering protection of minorities. It is important in any federal state to ensure that the central government is entrusted with parental obligations towards minority groups within the country[23]. The central government should be empowered and obligated by the constitution to take actions against states as appropriate for the sake of minority protection. This is not the case with the draft provisions proposed for new constitution. Though the central government has power to direct the provincial governments, this power has nothing to do with minority protection. Hence, consideration should be given for creating a concrete mechanism(e.g. Special Official/Rapporteur/Commissioner/Ombudsman) in the new Constitution to monitor, on regular basis, the situation of minorities and advise the central government.

Independent Judicial Check

Independent and competent judiciary is one of the perquisites for the effective protection of human rights. This is also an important element in any federation. There often remains a desperate need of an "independent and effective judicial check against executive and legislative excesses" at all levels of the government within a federal system. Independence of the judiciary is achieved through ensuring "actual independence of the Judiciary from the executive branch and the legislative".[24] However, article 29 (2) (a) of the CA Committee on the Judiciary's draft proposes to shift the authority for determining the constitutionality of laws from the Supreme Court to a parliamentary committee. This is very problematic in terms of human rights as it would not provide for an independent control on parliamentary actions encroaching upon fundamental rights. It is obvious that if the central legislature has the finality of decision in this regard, it ceases to be a federal system, because in the end the centre determines the interpretation of the constitution and consequently the powers of the regional units. Nepal also

---

[23] For instance, article 350 of Indian Constitution has created a Special Officer to monitor the situation of minorities and report to the President. Similarly, article 25 of the Constitutional Act of Canada obligates the government to promote and protect educational rights of the linguistic minorities in Canada. Article 153(b) of the Malaysian Constitution also entrust the Government with responsibility to safeguard the interest of natives.

[24] See, HRC General Comment on Article 2 of the ICCPR, and Principle 1 of the Basic Principles on Independence of Judiciary, 1984.

has international legal obligation to ensure the right to effective remedy by competent and independent courts under a number of international human rights treaties including the ICCPR[25]. It is noticeable that the original proposal of the CA Committee on Judiciary to sift the 'constitutional review power' from Supreme Court to a parliamentary committee appears to have been redundant with a developing political consensus to go for an option of independent judicial mechanism, within the framework of independence of judiciary, to give finality of decision on constitutional issues. However, there still remains a debate on whether it should be a supreme court with a constitutional bench or a separate constitutional court. Amidst, there has been a proposal to create an interim Constitutional Court for a period of 5 years to look after federalism related disputes. It appears that this has been designed without a judicial review power. As this 'interim court option' doesn't correspond to the need of smooth implementation of the federal system and protection and promotion of human rights including Economic, Social and Civil Rights (ESCR), consideration should be given to retaining the Supreme Court with the more specialized constitutional review function. Alternatively, a separate Constitutional Court entrusting a fully-fledged constitutional review function may also be considered in case there is no consensus on the retention of the Supreme Court with fully fledged constitutional review power.[26] At the same time, it is important for the new constitution to decentralize its writ jurisdiction together with power to entertain Public Interest Litigation (PIL) at appellate/high court level.

National Human Rights Institutions

The CA Committee on Constitutional Bodies has proposed for creating 11 constitutional commissions. Among the proposed commissions, seven such commissions including pre-existing National Human Rights Commission, by and large, relate to protection and promotion of human rights. Given the Nepalese experience to date in relation to the national human rights institutions, it is desirable to adopt a pragmatic approach, meaning that it is

---

[25] Article 2(3) of the ICCPR obliges the State to ensure that the right to a remedy is determined by competent judicial,legal or administrative authorities'.

[26] Article 167(3) of the South African Constitution, 1996.

useful to go for a few powerful, independent and competent commissions with a comprehensive mandate rather than creating many toothless (symbolic or without ability for effective performance) institutions. One viable option could be to go for retaining preexisting commissions (National Human Rights Commission (*NHRC*), *National Women's Commission (NWC) and National Dalit Commission (NDC)*) together with creation of an additional one- "Equality, Non-Discrimination and Inclusion Commission" - with a comprehensive mandate to look into discrimination, exclusion and marginalization. As long standing discrimination, exclusion and marginalization have been pointed out as reasons for creating such additional group specific Commissions, it may be logical to envision such a cross-cutting Commission and give it a comprehensive mandate to receive and investigate into complaints regarding the denial of non-discrimination and equality rights and make binding recommendations to all levels of the governments, as appropriate. Consideration can also be given to expand the effective presence of such Commissions at the provincial and local levels. While defining mandate, mode of appointment and the jurisdiction of these Commissions, it is important to comply with "The Paris Principles" (Principles Relating to the Status of National Human Rights Institutions, 1993).

Mere creation of these Commissions doesn't carry any value if their credibility and independence is compromised. Looking at the draft text related to National Human Rights Commission, many of the proposed provisions seem flawed in light of the Paris Principles[27]. Firstly, the proposed provisions do not adequately ensure representative and pluralistic form of the Commission as required by the Principles. The Paris Principles require national human rights institutions to be represented by all social forces, in particular representatives of non-governmental organizations, trade unions, and professional organizations, trends in philosophical and religious thought, and universities and qualified experts.[28] It is recognized that a national human rights institution which is diverse and pluralist can help guarantee its

---

[27] Principles relating to the Status of National Institutions ("Pans Principles"), adopted by General Assembly resolution 48/134, 20 December 2003

[28] See, Paris Principles, Principle 1 on "Composition and guarantees of independence and pluralism".

independence from governmental officials and bodies.[29] Instead of having a generic reference to "basis of proportionate representation and inclusiveness", the new constitution should therefore explicitly require the NHRC to have appropriate gender, social, ethnic and cultural representation so as to ensure that women, Dalits, the indigenous communities are represented in the commission.

Secondly, it is also equally important to have a representative/inclusive body as the key committee to make recommendations concerning the appointment of members of the NHRC. The current process of the President appointing on the advice of a Constitutional Council dominated by the Executive may not be seen as meeting this goal as such appointments may have the potential to undermine the independence of a national human rights commission.[30] Such a body might be a specifically constituted body with a combination of civil society representation, Government representation and Parliamentary representation, which could serve the purpose of maximizing the pluralist representation as required by the Paris Principles.

As the method by which members of a national human rights institution are appointed can be critical in ensuring its independence,[31] a representative body (e.g. parliament) could be entrusted with the responsibility to undertake the appointments process, in broad consultation with civil society.[32]However, there is no stipulation for a consultation or for the possibility of public nominations. Such a process cannot meet the purpose of maximising the pluralist representation, as required by the Paris Principles, and will inevitably lead to questions regarding the independence and credibility of the Commissioners.

---

[29] OHCHR Handbook on "National Human Rights Institutions: the Establishment and Strengthening of National Institutions for the Promotion and Protection of Human Rights" (OHCHR Handbook"), 1995, paragraph 82.

[30] International Coordinating Committee Paper; page 3.

[31] OHCHR Handbook, paragraph 79.

[32] OHCHR Handbook, paragraph 79; and "Appointments Procedures of National Human Rights Institutions", paper for the discussion of the International Coordinating Committee of National Human Rights Commissions ("International Coordinating Committee paper"), 13 April 2006, page4

Thirdly, the proposed provision concerning the NHRC's jurisdiction in relation to the army is also ambiguous. On the one hand, it provides that matters under the Army Act are not within the jurisdiction of the NHRC, on the other, it states that this is not a bar to proceedings concerning human rights or humanitarian law violations. This matter should be clarified in the new Constitution, to ensure that the NHRC is fully able to look into all alleged human rights violations, regardless of which State officials is responsible, including all army officers and personnel.

Fourthly, the proposed text doesn't empower the NHRC to appoint its own staff. The Paris Principles require a NHRC to have its own staff[33], in order to be independent of the government, and to further ensure its impartiality and credibility. Similarly, the General Comments of the International Coordinating Committee's Sub-Committee on Accreditation also emphasize that: *"As a principle, NHRIs should be empowered to appoint their own staff."* The new constitution should thus empower the NHRC to appoint its staff—including its Secretary – to ensure its operational independence and to be able to appoint staff with the relevant professional skills and experience.

Finally, there is no provision at all in the draft text referring to the funding of the Commission. In order to ensure that the NHRC functions effectively, financial autonomy should also be constitutionally guaranteed. The Paris Principles require an NHRI to have adequate funding and that "the purpose of this funding should be to enable [the NHRI] to have its own staff and premises, in order to be independent of the Government and not be subject to financial control which might affect its independence".[34] It is useful for the Constitution to include a provision ensuring that the NHRC is funded adequately and be able to exercise financial autonomy. Such explicit

---

[33] "...the purpose of this funding should be to enable it to have its own staff and premises, in order to be independent of the Government and not be subject to financial control which might affect its independence". [Paris Principles, 'Composition and guarantees of independent and pluralism'. point 2]

[34] See Paris Principles, Composition and guarantees of independece and pluralism, principle 2 ('The national institution shall have an infrastructure, which is suited to the smooth conduct of its activities, in particular adequate funding. The purpose of this funding should be to enable it to have its own staff and premises. in order to beindependent of the Government and not be subject to financial control which might affect its indepence").

provision particularly allows the NHRC the level of control necessary to ensure its' operational independence as well as greater financial autonomy in its daily operations.

It would also be preferable for the new constitution to include a provision that specifies the duty of the government and other state authorities to cooperate with the NHRC, with powers of sanction, such as administrative penalties, against state officials who fail to properly cooperate with the NHRC in the exercise of its mandate, through non-compliance, obstruction, interference or retaliation.[35]

Transitional Justice, Accountability and Impunity

It is impossible to secure sustainable peace within any federal state without developing a culture of accountability replacing the culture of impunity entrenched in the society. It is therefore important for the new constitution to pave the way for addressing past human rights violations and guaranteeing non-repetition of serious violations in future. Though the draft provision directs the government to adopt a number of reparation measures for the victims of past movements and revolutions, there has not been any provision retaining the Interim constitution's provisions[36] requiring the government to establish transitional justice mechanisms including Truth and Reconciliation Commission (TRC) and Disappearance commission. Given the fact that there has not been substantive progress towards advancing the transitional justice mechanisms as required by the Interim Constitution, consideration should be given to retaining the provision that requires the government set transitional justice mechanisms including TRC and Disappearance Commission consistent with international standards and

---

[35] Best Practices for NHRIs at 21: NHRIs should have the power to effectively address non-cooperation, obstruction, or victimisation in an investigation, e.g. a refusal to produce evidence. For examples of such provisions, see 35 of the National Human Rights Commission Act 1999 (Thailand).

[36] Article 33 (q) and (s) of the Interim Constitution respectively: "to provide relief to the families of the victims, on the basis of the report of the Investigation Commission constituted to investigate the cases of persons who were the subject of enforced disappearance during the course of the conflict, to constitute a high-level Truth and Reconciliation Commission to investigate the facts about those persons involved in serious violations of human rights and crimes against humanity committed during the course of conflict, and to create an atmosphere of reconciliation in the society."

best practices. In addition to paving the way for Transitional Justice mechanisms, the new constitution should address long-standing culture of impunity through prohibiting amnesty, pardon, case withdrawal and military justice in the context of serious violations of international human rights and humanitarian laws.

The draft text at present contains a blanket prohibition on retrospective criminal laws. Whilst this guarantee is also contained in the ICCPR, in the ICCPR there is an explicit exception covering acts or omissions 'which at the time when it was committed, was criminal according to the general principles of law recognized by the community of nations' (Article 15, ICCPR). This is an important exception which permits action to be taken in relation to international crimes and should be inserted into the Constitution. there was no criminalization of 'enforced disappearance' during the conflict, if 'laws' is restricted to referring to domestic criminal laws, the constitution would seem to impose a barrier on the retroactive application of a new enforced disappearances criminal provision. Therefore, Article 5(4) should be amended to allow for an exception of retrospective criminal law dealing with serious crimes under international law including genocide, crime against humanity, war crimes, enforced disappearance and torture.

The proposed pardoning provision also entrusts the President with a sweeping authority on pardoning and clemency. There has not been any provision that bars *de facto* and *de jure* amnesties including pardon in the context of serious crimes including enforced disappearance, torture and rape. Under several human rights treaties and U.N. principles and guidelines that reflect "existing legal obligations under international law," States may not grant amnesty for gross violations of human rights, which include but are not limited to torture and enforced disappearance.[37] Amnesties for gross violations of human rights may also violate States' obligations under customary law. Consideration should be given to ensuring that a provision concerning the granting of measures of clemency should be subject to the

---

[37] Basic Principles and Guidelines on the Right to a Remedy and Reparation for Victims of Gross Violations of International Human Rights Law and Serious Violations of International Humanitarian Law, preamble, G.A. Res. 60/147; see International Covenant on Civil and Political Rights, American Convention on Human Rights, African Charter on Human and Peoples' Rights, and European Convention for the Protection of Human Rights and Fundamental Freedoms, including related commentary and jurisprudence.

overall responsibility of the State to fulfill victims' rights of truth, justice and reparations. Ensuring accountability for serious crimes through baring amnesty and measures of clemency is very important, given the context of transitional justice processes that are supposed to deal with the past human rights violation and guaranteeing non-repetition of such violations in the future. Therefore, it is recommended that the constitution explicitly provides for impermissibility of de jure and de facto amnesties including pardon and withdrawal of criminal charges for serious crimes including enforced disappearance, torture, murder and rape.

Similarly, the proposed provision doesn't ensure a transparent and impartial system of accountability as this doesn't define the scope of the Special Military Court. From international human rights law perspective, there has been suggestion that all arms of the government including the security forces (army, police and armed police) are subject to ordinary processes of law. As suggested by UN Updated Set of Principles (2005) in relation to Impunity[38], it would be preferable for the Constitution to have an explicit provisionclarifying that the jurisdiction of civilian courts shall apply to all ordinary offences committed by military personnel (meaning that the special military tribunal is limited to purely military offences only). This is also a matter of the right of victims of human rights violations to have effective remedy from an independent and competent court guaranteed under article 2 of the ICCPR. In this regard, article 29 of the Constitution of Venezuela sets an example in terms of recognizing the civilian courts' control over military courts.[39]

Justifiability of Economic, Social and Civil Rights (ESCR)

The preliminary draft text regarding fundamental rights and directive principles proposes for wider stipulation of the ESC guarantees. Compared to the Interim Constitution, it provides for additional rights including right to housing.

---

[38] The principle 29 reads, "The jurisdiction of military tribunals must be restricted solely to specifically military offences committed by military personnel, to the exclusion of human rights violations, which shall come under the jurisdiction of the ordinary domestic courts or, where appropriate, in the case of serious crimes under international law, of an international or internationalized criminalcourt."

[39] The provision reads, "Human rights violations and the offense of violating humanity rights shall be investigated and adjudicated by the courts of ordinary competence."

In addition, many of the ESC rights provisions under the Interim Constitution have been revised to ensure precision. However, justifiability of the ESCR remains a challenge as under the Interim Constitution.

Clause 31(1) of the draft text creates a separate legal regime for economic, social and cultural rights and Clause 31(2) provides a two years time frame for making legal arrangements required for the implementation of the fundamental rights. These types of provisions are not useful and appropriate unless their application is specific to a particular component of the rights which need to have legal arrangements. As the current provision seems not specific to particular right, these would have potential to be counterproductive, undermining the enforceability of ESCR guarantees. Though the draft text provides for additional ESC rights including the right to housing compared to the Interim Constitution and many of the ESC rights provisions under the Interim Constitution have been revised to ensure precision, the ESCR guarantees are likely to be reduced to statutory guarantees by virtue of the clause 31 (1) (2), if and when legislature chooses to enact relevant legislation.

As denial of ESCR is widely accepted as one of the root causes of the conflict in Nepal, there should be no compromise in terms of ensuring ESCRs in a justiciable way on equal footing to the civil and political rights. A viable alternative to the scheme proposed by the Committee is a constitutional provision that eensures an immediate enforceability of "minimum core elements" of ESCR, consistent with developing national and international jurisprudence, make other elements of ESCR subject to "progressive realization obligation" in a justiciable way and prohibits any retrogression in area of ESCR. In case consideration is given to providing a time-bound obligation in terms of the enforcement of certain rights, it would be preferable for the new constitution to discern the components of rights that requires a legislative enactment to make them enforceable, rather than providing for generic application of this clause.[40]

---

[40] For instance, the South African constitution provides for a time-bound obligation to enact laws in relation to specific components of the Bill of Rights including Section 9(4). Section 23(1) of Schedule 6 (Transitional Arrangement) reads," National legislation envisioned in sections 9(4), 32(2) and 33(3) of the new constitution must be enacted within three years of the date on which the new constitution took effect."

Strengthening Equality Clause

Right to equality is cross-cutting for all civil, political, economic, social and cultural rights-whether they are in form of a collective or an individual right. Strengthened equality clause, therefore, would have a significant impact upon enjoyment of all human rights including ESCR within the federation. Compared to the "equality clause" under the Interim Constitution, some progress has been made in the Preliminary draft text. The positive developments in relation to the equality clause include:

- Prohibition of discrimination based on additional grounds (e.g. disability, marital status, sexual orientation and economic status).

- Open-ended list of the prohibited grounds of discrimination, which allows inclusion of other grounds through judicial interpretation in future.

- Coverage of equal "benefit" of law alongside equal "protection" of law.

However, there still remain a significant number of gaps and weaknesses yet to be addressed. Such weaknesses, in particular, include; lacking explicit prohibition of indirect discrimination (CRPD also requires such prohibition), lack of horizontal application of the non-discrimination/ equality clause (CRPD requires; South African constitution provides for) and failure to ensure right to substantive equality.

It is, therefore, recommended to make sure that the direct and indirect forms of discrimination are prohibited, the right to non-discrimination is applied in a vertical (against the state) as well as horizontal way (against the non-state actors/Individuals as well), the "substantive equality" is guaranteed and the scope of "special measures clause" is clarified.

Application of International Human Rights Law

Nepal is a party to more than two dozen international human rights treaties. However, the status of international treaties in national legal system remains ambiguous.However the Interim Constitution, in its Chapter on Responsibilities of the State, does refer to the State obligation to implement effectively the international treaties and agreements to which Nepal is a party.[41] This provision is yet to be interpreted, especially with respect to how this responsibility should be carried out. It should be noted, however, that this provision is found in a Chapter which includes another provision stating that no issues about implementation of the obligations are to be raised in any court. The ongoing constitution making process can be utilized as an opportunity to clarify the status. Just sifting the Section 9 of Nepal Treaty Act into the constitution does not address the problem (as proposed by the Committee on National Interest). This provision is proposed to provide for the post-ratification effect of the treaties in Nepal. This provision will have an effect of making some treaty provisions applicable in particular circumstances, namely where there is a conflict between those provisions of international law and Nepali law (doesn't include constitutional provisions). Except in the stated circumstances, the provisions of international treaties which Nepal has ratified donot automatically form part of Nepalese law unless and until those provisions have been validly incorporated into domestic law by statute. On the other, the treaty provisions conflicted with the constitutional provisions are not applicable unless "Nepali law" is defined to include constitutional law.

Therefore, it order to provide for the maximum protection of human rights, consideration might be given to securing explicit constitutional stipulations obligating the courts to interpret law and constitution in compliance with international human rights law (e.g. South Africa).This can be further strengthened by providing a reference requiring adopting appropriate measures including legislative, executive, judicial and administrative as appropriate. Comparative experiences from Kosovo [42]

---

[41] Interim Constitution of Nepal, article 33(m).

[42] Article 22 of the Kosovo Constitution 2008 : Human rights and fundamental freedoms guaranteed by the following international agreements and instruments are guaranteed by this Constitution, are directly applicable in the Republic of Kosovo and, in the case of conflict, have priority over provisions of laws and other acts of public institutions: (1) Universal Declaration of Human Rights; (2) European Convention for the Protection of Human Rights and Fundamental Freedoms and its Protocols; (3) International Covenant on Civil and Political Rights and its Protocols; (4) Council of Europe Framework Convention for the Protection of National Minorities; (5) Convention on the Elimination of All Forms of Racial Discrimination; (6) Convention on the Elimination of All Forms of Discrimination Against Women; (7) Convention on the Rights of the Child; (8) Convention against Torture and Other Cruel, Inhumane or Degrading Treatment or Punishment.

and Argentina[43] could also be useful in case a consideration is given to insert a provision allowing for direct application of some human rights treaties.

Citizenship

By virtue of the proposed provisions, the Nepali citizens married to foreign nationals are unable to pass on their citizenship to their children. In another word, unless both father and mother are Nepali citizens, the children born to Nepali citizens married to foreigners are not entitled to have Nepali citizenship. If such a criteria that "both parents are Nepali citizens at the time of birth" is stipulated, this will be a reverse progress in terms of citizenship rights as article 8(2)(b) of the Interim Constitution provides for any person to have a right to citizenship if either of his/her parents is Nepali citizen at the time of birth. Therefore, the proposed provisions appear to be resulted in reduction of the rights of children, who may at present acquire nationality through either of parents. This is also a concern in terms of Nepal's obligations under a number of human rights treaties to which Nepal is a party[44]. Consideration, therefore, should be given to amending these provisions so that an individual whose mother or father was a Nepalese citizen during his/her birth is entitled to Nepali citizenship. It is also important to make sure that there would be no any discrimination on the basis of

---

[43] Article 75 (22) of the Argentinean Constitution (1994 Amendments): To approve or reject treaties concluded with other nations and international organizations, and concordats with the Holy See. Treaties and concordats have a higher hierarchy than laws: The American Declaration of the Rights and Duties of Man; the Universal Declaration of Human Rights; the American Convention on Human Rights; the International Pact on Economic, Social and Cultural Rights; the International Pact on Civil and Political Rights and its empowering Protocol; the Convention on the Prevention and Punishment of Genocide; the International Convention on the Elimination of all Forms of Racial Discrimination; the Convention on the Elimination of all Forms of Discrimination against Woman; the Convention against Torture and other Cruel, Inhuman or Degrading Treatments or Punishments; the Convention on the Rights of the Child; in the full force of their provisions, they have constitutional hierarchy, do no repeal any section of the First Part of this Constitution and are to be understood as complementing the rights and guarantees recognized herein. They shall only be denounced, in such event, by the National Executive Power after the approval of two-thirds of all the members of each House. In order to attain constitutional hierarchy, the other treaties and conventions on human rights shall require the vote of two-thirds of all the members of each House, after their approval by Congress.

[44] The obligations present in the ICCPR, CERD, and CRC require Nepal to ensure that children within the territory of a State party are not made stateless. Notably, the ICCPR not only recognizes that all children have the right to a nationality (Article 24), it establishes an affirmative obligation on the part of State parties to take measures—including the passage of appropriate laws—to give full effect to this right (Article 2(2)).

gender. As the right to non-discrimination and equality regardless of gender is immutable under international legal standards enforceable on Nepal, citizenship can't be an exception. It is, therefore, important to ensure gender equality in terms prescribing setting constitutional criteria on acquisition, transfer, renunciation and termination of the citizenship.

Final Observation

As the constitution making process offers a wonderful opportunity for Nepal to write its fundamental law consistent with universal principles of democracy and human rights, there should be no hesitation to strengthen constitutional protection of human rights in light of Nepal's international human rights obligations. Many of the shortcomings of the proposals for new constitution may be addressed into line with the universally accepted standards of human rights. As the Supreme Court of Nepal says that the international human rights treaties are "scriptures of modern era" *(Rina Bazracharya Case)*, they can be best utilized not only to strengthen bill of rights under the new constitution but also in terms of seeking human rights friendly solution to many of the contentious issues pertaining to federalism.

Security Provisions in a Federal Future

Chiran Jung Thapa

Nepal had remained a unitary state for more than two hundred thirty years.[1] That status quo changed following a proclamation on May 28, 2008. On this date, Nepal was declared a Federal Democratic Republic by the first sitting of the constituent Assembly. This proclamation, however, has only conferred a federal title to the polity. Four years have elapsed since that proclamation, and a federal structure is yet to be institutionalized. More so, with the abysmal failure of the Constituent Assembly to promulgate the constitution after repeated tenure extensions, Nepal's stride towards a federal future remains forestalled.

The demand for federalism in Nepal stems primarily from a long-standing aspirations for self-governance in regions outside the centre (Kathmandu). Those dwelling in the periphery have long deemed the existing state apparatus as unresponsive and distant. It was the Maoists that capitalized on these aspirations of the ignored and the oppressed constituencies. The armed insurrection launched by the Maoists inadvertently boosted the federal agenda. The Maoists shrewdly peddled the idea of granting federal autonomy to entice those grievous groups into joining their campaign. Actually, the forty point demand that was submitted to the government of the time by the Maoists hints towards federalism. Although there is no explicit mention of federalism, the demand for decentralisation

---

[1] Since the foundation of the Nepal in 1768 by Late King Prithvi Narayan Shah until Nepal was declared a "Federal Democratic Republic" in 2007, Nepal had remained a unitary State

in real terms in which local areas would have local rights, autonomy and control over their own resources was an integral part of their demand.[2]

It was the Madesh uprising of 2007 that actually provided the most powerful thrust to propel the polity towards federalism. In fact, Gajendra Narayan Singh – a prominent Madheshi leader of the Nepal Sadbhavana party had broached the federalist agenda during the early nineties.[3] That, however, fizzled or was somehow overshadowed by other political developments until the Madhesh uprising in 2007. The Madheshi movement blaringly demonstrated the Madhesi people's aspirations for autonomy and self rule. It was through this movement that the slogan for "one Madhesh one Pradesh" became pronounced and the agenda of federalism came to the forefront.

The eclectic proponents of federalism have based their demands for a federal configuration upon three imperatives. First, it is the recognition and empowerment of ethnic identities. Second, self rule through the devolution of power from central to the local level. Third is the right over resources and economic viability. Whether these three imperatives are taken individually or in conglomeration, the crystallizing element is the belief that these can be attained through a federal structure, and that the new setup would provide more empowerment and security.

In order to realize the federal aspiration of the varying constituencies, a State Restructuring Commission comprised of experts was commissioned in November of 2011. The task was to advise the government on the optimal configuration of federal units. The members of this Commission were a diverse lot. They represented various political parties and were of different ethnic backgrounds. They, however, could not come to a consensus over the formation of new provincial units. Following the disagreement amongst the member of the commission, two separate reports were submitted to the government.[4] The first report submitted by the majority faction had suggested

---

[2] Deepak Thapa and Bandita Sijapati (eds), *A Kingdom Under Siege: Nepal's Maoists Insurgence, 1996 to 2003*. 2003, (Kathmandu: The Printhouse, 2003), 192.

[3] Many commentaries on federalism have mentioned about Gajendra Narayan Singh's role in bringing the agenda of federalism in the limelight.

[4] See *Kantipur* of 1 February 2012.

11 federal units namely Karnali-Khaptad, Madhes-Abadh-Tharuwan, Magrat, Tamuwan, Narayani, Newa, Tamsaling, Kirat, Limbuwan, Madhes-Mithila-Bhojpura and one non-territorial Dalit state. The other report submitted by the minority faction had called for the government to form six provincial structures, two in the plains (Terai) based on identity and culture and four in hills and mountains on the basis of economic viability.

Although the basis of demarcation of provincial units is a highly contentious issue as illustrated by the separate Commission reports, one thing, however, is indisputable. New security provisions in the newly formed provinces are mandatory and that it will need to be more robust than the pre-existing provisions. It would be counter intuitive to maintain that constituencies in the newly formed provinces will desire environments that are less secure than the pre-existing ones. The demand for a federal setup is actually a direct result of the convictions that the new set up will grant them more rights over their fates which would in turn result in a more secure environment. Not only that, given the contentions, the provincial units will need to make even better security arrangements to ensure that the contentions don't flare up into violent conflicts.

Prior to delving into the security provisions in a federal future, however, it is equally important to delve into the concept of security. In today's globalized, interconnected and interdependent environment, the realm of security is no longer confined to the traditionalist view. In fact, there has been a huge paradigm shift in the concept of security. In the past, the term security had a military connotation and implied an element of force. During the cold war, the threats that dictated the security agenda were predominantly military in nature and it emanated from beyond the national boundaries. Following the end of the cold war, Military threats have become less of a concern. Instead, other threats such as terrorism, global warming, natural/manmade disasters, nuclear proliferation, health endemics, resource depletion, that are complex, asymmetric and trans-national in nature have become more of a challenge. Also, the State-centric security agenda is slowly evolving into a human-security priority as economic, social, environmental and even psychological variables are being innately intertwined with the concept of security.

Given the broad discourse of security coupled with the national limitations on realizing this ideal, and the provided parameters for this paper, this paper will deliberately omit these unconventional security realms and only discuss the "hard security[5]" provisions. Through this paper, the author will seek to briefly highlight some of the necessary security provisions to secure Nepal's federal future. The paper will also gloss over the status quos of the security agencies in a federal setup.

A Constitution

The drafting and promulgation of the constitution is perhaps the most vital task in realizing a federal set up. Constitutions are generally the supreme law of the land. No other law supersedes it. As the supreme document, it provides the necessary guidelines and delineations of powers and limitations for security provisions of a country. First, the constitution decrees the names, powers, functions and responsibilities of the Central government and the putative federal units. It also specifies the electoral processes and system of governance. Second, it lists the national interests that are vital for the existence of Nepal. By pronouncing the national interests, the constitution provides guidance to devise other subordinate laws, policies and strategies regarding security provisions. Alongside, the criminal justice system derives its laws in abidance to the constitution. The fundamental rights of citizen residing within the state too are enshrined in the constitution. In regards to security provisions, the state's ability to shield its citizens from the scourge of war is important. Constitutions also generally lay out the provisions about an act of war/ declaring war. The provisions regarding components such as role and deployment of armed forces that would fight the war, the powers of decision makers that decide to declare and go to war are generally all laid out in the constitution.

A National Security Policy

Irrespective of the system of governance, the primary function of the government of any state is to provide security to its citizens. There is no other responsibility that supersedes this responsibility. In fact, the social

---

[5] The term "hard security" refers to provisions requiring the use of force.

contract between the government and governed is derived from the consent between the denizens that subordinate themselves to the law of the state and the government that reciprocates by providing security.[6]

Therefore, following the promulgation of the Constitution, another document that is vital in securing the nation and its people is a comprehensive National Security Policy (NSP). The constitution may or may or explicitly spell out about the national security policy. Regardless, however, the promulgation of a constitution provides the necessary elements required to draft a NSP. The constitution is generally a nationally revered and owned document that enlists the national interests and responsibilities of actors and agencies governing the state. Taking into account these very unwavering national interests of the nation, a NSP is drafted in accordance.

NSP is generally a broad political vision which describes how a nation will provide security for the State and its citizens. This policy highlights the nation's place in the geo-political order. It also outlines the national interest and objectives and mentions of the strategies to be employed to protect, and preserve those national interests that the state deems are vital for the existence of the nation and the security and the welfare of its citizens. Alongside, Strengths, Weaknesses, Threats and Opportunities (SWOT) are analyzed, and roles of actors/agencies are defined and coordination between these actors are outlined.

The question in a federal setup would be - who drafts the NSP? The task of drafting a NSP generally rests on the central government. This practice is universally accepted. A national security apparatus that is called a National Security Council (NSC) is established at the central level. The composition of the NSC varies. The head of the government chairs this council and has other members of the cabinet such as ministers of home affairs, foreign affairs, defense and finance as members of this council. The Chiefs of security agencies could also be members of this council. Other members could include senior members of the bureaucracy and sometimes an advisory panel could also be embedded as part of the council.

---

[6] Wrong Orders, *The Kathmandu Post*, 13 January 2012.

Also, equally important is the issue over how much influence individual federal units would yield over the drafting of the NSP. The influence could vary. However, what is certain is that the NSP would in one manner or the other require the endorsement of the provincial units. Therefore, the security perceptions and concerns of the units will somehow be accommodated in the NSP.

Nepal at the moment does not have a NSP. Through the years, numerous drafts have been drafted by various actors and entities but none has been unanimously endorsed and or has come into effect. As a consequence, the National Security agenda has always remained in the backburner. Further, a National Security Council Secretariat (NSC) secretariat has existed for a number of years. Its function, however, has been hobbled by the blithe ignorance of the political forces in power. The underlying disinterest on issues of national security has rendered an inconspicuous existence of the NSC secretariat. Therefore, it continues to remain as the dumping ground for members of the security agencies.[7]

Military (Nepal Army)

The existing provisions regarding the National Army as stipulated in the interim constitution will most likely remain unaltered in a federal setup. As is the case with almost all countries federal or not, national militaries are directly under the jurisdiction of the central government. Its formation and function are generally outlined in the constitution. As is the function of any military, Nepal Army (NA)'s conventional function would be to defend and deter any hostile incursion into national boundaries by any external force. However, in Peace times, its roles could vary. Currently, NA is deployed for multiple purposes. International Peacekeeping, rescue and relief operations during natural calamities, national infrastructure building, VIP security, security of certain national installations, and forest and wildlife conservation remain some of the current NA's engagements. It was also engaged in counter insurgency operations from 2001 to 2006.

---

[7] Members of Nepal Army, APF, Nepal Police and NID are all working at the NSC secretariat. Officers from these agencies do not consider a position in the NSC as a plum position. Instead, it is considered the dumping ground.

The only foreseeable change could be the size of the current force and possibly slashing of some peace time roles. NA almost doubled in size following its engagement in counter insurgency operations. Today, close to 93,000 serve in this organization. There have been calls from several quarters for its downsizing citing that the country cannot bear the economic burden of sustaining a large Army. However, simply slashing size whimsically would be unfounded. Instead, a thorough Defense Review that would carefully analyze the existing and future threats and capabilities and then determine the force ratio in accordance is imperative. Such a review could also help determine which non traditional roles to discontinue and what other requirements are necessary to maximize the operational readiness for a conventional role.

Intelligence (National Investigation Department)

Intelligence is a product, process and a profession that is innately intertwined with National Security. Unlike other states that truly value of the role of intelligence and their intelligence agencies, Nepal's governance structures and psyche have never reflected that inclination. Although Nepal does have an intelligence agency, many seem unaware about its existence. There could be multiple reasons behind this ignorance. It could easily be the title of the organization (National Investigation Department) and the titles of those working for the organization that make it seem like another Police agency and not an intelligence agency. The rank structure is almost identical to that of regular police. The nature of its work which mainly comprises of internal eavesdropping also makes the NID seem like a detective agency. Currently, this agency is under the Ministry of Home Affairs.

In Nepal's federal future, what role would such an agency play? If the existing agency is maintained or a separate entity is ordained with the task of conducting intelligence work, then, like most countries with a federal setup, the Intelligence agency will have to remain under the central government. Similar to the Central Intelligence Agency (CIA) of the United States and the Research and Analysis Wing (R&AW), this agency would remain directly under the head of the government. Second, like any other intelligence agency, its functions would be to ensure that there are no strategic surprises by timely forecasting developments, events, forces and threats.[8]

Also, it would provide support to the policy process through tailored and timely intelligence and maintain the secrecy of information, needs and methods. An updated and refined act would be necessary to provide guidance to such an agency.[9]

Paramilitary (Armed Police Force)

Nepal's paramilitary outfit – the Armed Police force (APF) was established in 2001 to combat the Maoist insurgency. Citing the inability of the existing Police force to quell the insurgency coupled with the complexities involved in deploying the national Military, this new outfit was erected. Within a decade of its birth, this outfit has managed to almost triple in size. Under the Ministry of Home Affairs, the strength of APF today stands at 31,265.

Unlike the NA, it is quite unclear as to what would become of this outfit in a federal setup. While some have called for it remain intact under the central government and continue with its current mandate, others have gone to the extreme of calling for its disbandment or merger into the Nepal Police.

The decision on its fate, however, will need to be made with several considerations. First, the utility of such a force needs to be questioned. What mandate would such a paramilitary unit have during peace time? Second, if there is clarity over its mandate, then the optimal size of the force needs to be ascertained. Third, special consideration needs to be accorded to the availability of financial resources for such a unit. Fourth, duplication of roles and missions that clash with other security agencies need to be avoided. However, from its current composition and ability, the future role of this unit could be best suited for border security, deployment for internal emergencies ranging from armed insurrection to natural disasters and riot control. Just like other paramilitaries, this unit will need to remain under the jurisdiction of the central government.

---

[8] Mark Lowenthal Mark, *Intelligence from secrets to policy*, (Washington D.C.:CQ press, 2003), 2-4.

[9] Ibid

Police (Nepal Police)

Perhaps the organization that could be most affected by federalism is Nepal Police (NP). Currently, the NP with the strength of 60,000 is a national organization under the Ministry of Home Affairs is the primary law enforcement agency.

In a federal future, the provincial units will most likely opt for local police units under their jurisdiction. Therefore, NP could potentially be divided amongst the new federal units. The jurisdiction of the new units under such a setup will likely change but the primary functions, however, will remain unaltered. Crime prevention, law enforcement, investigation, traffic management will continue to remain the top functions of most local police units.

Retaining some form of central police unit would be propitious for a federal setup for multiple reasons. Like the CBI in India and FBI in the US, Nepal may require a central police authority for several reasons. First, for training purposes and capacity building of federal police units, a central Police unit is vital. Since NP has a long history and substantial experience, a certain segment of the force could remain as the central unit under the central jurisdiction. Second, for crimes concerning cross-border issues like trafficking, organized crime, terrorism etc, jurisdiction and capacity of the local police units may be limited. Therefore, a central unit with those aforementioned capacities becomes imperative. Third, there is a need of a central unit to serve as a counterpart to other police forces around the world. For example, issues related to Interpol would require a central unit for coordination as it would be difficult to maintain individual contacts with so many local police units. Fourth, in the times of need for certain federal units, the central Police unit could serve as reinforcement.

Emergency Response Units

If hard security provisions are to be made truly robust in the new federal setup, each of the provincial units needs to be endowed with a capability to tackle emergency situations. Nepal endures natural calamities such as floods, landslides, fires and other emergencies on a regular basis. However, the response and relief capacity of the state is extremely weak as the existing security agencies are not designed to handle such contingencies. The emergency crew is usually mustered on an ad hoc need basis and such a crew is neither properly trained or has the necessary/proper wherewithal to deal with the dire contingency. Therefore, as important as the creation of new law enforcement units, the creation of independent emergency rescue and relief units in each of the federal units could prove to be propitious. Essentially, this force could be comprised of firefighters, divers, search and rescue crew, hazmat unit and medical units.

Finances

Security does not come free of cost. It requires significant financing for the lubrication and upkeep of the security apparatus. Therefore, whichever way the federal units are demarcated, the security provisions will require certain financing. Therefore, the allocation of resources for security provisions needs to be meticulously planned for. Given the diversity in topography and demography of this polity, no permutation would yield a balanced distribution of resources amongst the units. As a result, some units will be more endowed than the others. Usually, the security agencies under the central government such as the military, intelligence and paramilitary units are financed by the central government. Unless there are special considerations/ provisions, the responsibility of financing the local law enforcement agencies, state legislatures, state-level judiciary and bureaucracy all fall on the shoulders of the federal units themselves. Therefore, as financing provisions have direct correlation with security provisions, planning for finances is crucial.

Conclusion

With the dissolution of the Constituent Assembly, Nepal's march towards a federal future has momentarily come to a grinding halt. The inability of the political forces represented in the Constituent Assembly to come to a consensus about how the unitary state should be reconfigured caused the dissolution of the Assembly. Despite the dissolution, however, an alliance of political forces championing a federal setup has recently been formed. While on one side there are proponents that are vociferously demanding a federal future, the other side of the spectrum has a constituency that is bitterly against the idea of dividing up of the unitary state. Then, even those in the proponent camp remain divided as there is deep disagreement over the basis of demarcation. Thus, it is clearly evident that federal future of Nepal will be riddled with contentions. The contentions certainly have the potential to flare up and take a violent trajectory if the expectations and aspirations of divergent constituencies are not managed properly. Contentions aside, the way this agenda has treaded forward, it does appear that federalism in one format or the other is inevitable. As Nepal inches towards a federal fate, it would be judicious to begin planning for an effective institutionalization of federalism. More than anything, effective institutionalization of federalism would require meticulous security provisions. For, the only intersection of the proponents and the opponents of federalism is the underlying desire to ensure a safe and secure future in Nepal.

Conflict and its Economic Consequences in Nepal

Hari Bansh Jha

Background

For centuries, Nepal remained a peaceful nation. But the year 1996 proved a marked departure in the history of Nepal as the Communist Party of Nepal (Maoists) started 'People's War' in that year with a view to abolishing monarchy and establishing communist republic. They started the so called 'People's War' from one of the isolated pockets of Jajarkot, Rukum and Rolpa districts in western part of the hills and managed to influence most parts of the country, including the Terai region of Nepal bordering Indian states. Between 1996 and 2006, the Maoists claimed to have controlled over 80 per cent of the rural areas of Nepal. But the district headquarters and Kathmandu Valley largely remained out of the control of the Maoists.

The conflict proved over costly to Nepal. About 17,828 people were killed by the Maoists and the security forces.[1] This directly affected the lives of their 450,000 family members. Besides, more than 5,800 people were disabled, 25,000 children were orphaned, 9,000 women were widowed and 14,852 people were disappeared.[2] Properties of 11,000 persons were damaged.[3] Agriculture, industry and trade sectors were heavily affected. Many of the infrastructural facilities such as schools, government offices,

---

[1] RSS, "Displaced haven't received relief," *The Himalayan Times*, March 28, 2012 in http://www.thehimalayantimes.com/fullNews.php?headline=%27Displaced+haven%27t+r...

[2] Ibid.

[3] Hari Bansh Jha, "The Economics of Peace: A Nepalese Perspective" ORF OCCASIONAL PAPER#29, December 2011, New Delhi: Observer Research Foundation, p. 14.

hydro-electric plants, bridges and even temples were destroyed by the rebels.

Most of the people killed by the warring factions were young people belonging to the productive age group of 15-60. They could have made significant contribution in GDP if remained alive. There was a huge cost involved in the treatment of people physically and mentally tortured during the conflict period. Many of the women had to live in the environment of tension and financial insecurity as they lost their husbands or the ones who were the only source of support for them.[4] Estimates are that the 10 years long conflict pushed the country 30 years back and that it made the 30 million Nepalese still poorer.

Thanks to Indian mediation that the 12 point agreement was signed between the CPN (Maoists) and the Seven Political Parties of Nepal in November 2005. This paved the way for the signing of Comprehensive Peace Agreement between the CPN (Maoists) and the government of Nepal in 2006. After the signing of the Comprehensive Peace Agreement, some epoch-making events followed. The elections of the Constituent Assembly (CA) were completed in 2008. The 239 year old monarchical institution came to an end. Nepal was declared Federal Democratic Republic. Elections of President and Vice-President were performed. The CPN (Maoists) was able to form a coalition government under the Prime Ministership of Pushpa Kamal Dahal in 2008. But just within nine months after becoming Prime Minister, Dahal resigned from his post on May 4, 2009. Subsequently, a coalition government was formed under the Prime Ministership of Madhav Kumar Nepal and Jhalanath Khanal of Communist Party of Nepal- Unified Marxist-Leninist (CPN-UML) one after the other. And then, Baburam Bhattrai of CPN (Maoists) formed government with the support of Madhesh-based parties. But none of governments formed following the CA elections was able to form Truth and Reconciliation Commission as well as the Commission on the Disappeared persons, which is a great set back to peace process in Nepal.

---

[4] Bishnu P. Poudel and Hari Bansh Jha (Ed.) *The new Dynamics of Conflict in Nepal.* Kathmandu: The National Advisory Council-South Asian Affairs, The Center for Economic and Technical Studies in cooperation with Friedrich-Ebert-Stiftung, 2009, p. 25.

Economic Drivers of Conflict

It was not without reason why the conflict occurred in Nepal. First and foremost driving factor of conflict was the age-old ethnic, caste, regional and gender discrimination. The Maoists had raised certain issues in favour of the downtrodden sections of the society such as the Dalits, women and other marginalized groups. Besides, many of the downtrodden sections of the society, including the Dalits and Janajatis were suspected of supporting the rebel forces and as such they found it quite difficult to make an earning. Frequent *bandhs* during the period not only affected people's movement but it also adversely affected the food supplies due to the transport problems. The distortion in the supply of food from one part of the country to the other resulted in the rise in prices of foodgrains, which affected the lower–income group people most. Many of the Dalits and Janajatis were almost forced to join the rebel army because of the growing suspicion of the state towards them.

Moreover, most of the Non Governmental Organizations (NGOs) and International Non-Governmental Organizations (INGOs) working in the country raised people's expectations, but they contributed very little in terms of eradicating poverty. Aids and assistance received from the bilateral and multilateral institutions failed to address even the basic needs of the people. In fact, larger part of the aid and assistance benefited mostly the bureaucrats and those closer to power centre. But those people were cut off from the grass roots and were confined mostly to Kathmandu Valley and other urban areas. This gave ample opportunities to the rebel forces to thrive in the rural and remote parts of the country.

Growing unemployment among the youth was another driving force for conflict. Poverty, illiteracy and lack of development opportunities in areas like the roads, electricity and health facilities had created massive unemployment problem. The situation aggravated when many people lost their jobs due to the closure of industries. Many others lost livelihood as they could not run petty businesses, especially in the informal sector. Those poor people who depended on wages were hardest hit because of the lack of economic activities. Many people were thrown out of jobs in the industries, construction and even in agricultural sectors. A few of those who worked with government bodies, NGOs and INGOs lost their jobs as those organizations increasingly felt threatened to work in the field. Conflict largely affected the employment prospect and livelihood of many of the people. As a result, many of the unemployed youth had little option left but to join the rebel forces who provided them alternative source of livelihood.

At the initial stage, the Maoists launched different activities not only to remove such social problems as gambling, drinking and corruption but they also punished many moneylenders. They asked many of the NGOs and INGOs to become transparent while running their programmes in the rural areas. Some of those activities instilled a feeling in certain quarters that the Maoists would make a difference in the society and so they supported the party.

State Policy Aggravating Conflict

During the conflict period, the strikes, security checks, blockades and shutdowns were quite frequent. Besides, beatings, threatening, humiliation, forced unethical acts, social isolation, tying down, rape and sexual harassments were also common. Extra-judicial killings, disappearances, extortions and abductions of people were the order of the day. Quite often, the Maoists targeted police posts, army barracks, government offices and other security agencies. In such a time of crisis, the government made a policy whereby the police posts that were spread to the rural areas were withdrawn to the district headquarters. Even many of the government offices were shifted to the district headquarters. The Nepalese army rarely provided security to the people as they were largely confined to the barracks. During the time of conflict, when there was a need to increase the presence of police, army and other security agencies to the rural and remote parts of the country and use them against the rebel forces, the government withdrew them. This provided green pastures to the rebel forces in the Himalayan, hills and Terai regions to intensify their activities.

In addition, the government dissolved the all the local level bodies during the conflict period, which included Village Development Committees (VDCs), municipalities and District Development Committees (DDCs).

All those local units had representatives duly elected by the people. With the dissolution of those bodies, the government lost its hold at the local level in the villages, municipalities and the districts. The state largely proved failure in providing security to the people. In such a situation, the rebel forces targeted mostly the landowners, moneylenders, officials, traders and all those who opposed them mostly in the rural areas. Many of them were forced to provide food and shelter to the Maoists.

Villagers working abroad had a tough time to return back to their villages because there was often fear of forced donation and abductions. Often the young boys and girls were pressurized to join the Maoist army.[5] The social life was plagued as both the Maoists and security forces kept a close watch on the youth.

As many of the male population escaped from the villages to avoid conflict, the women became more vulnerable in the rural areas. In several villages, virtually there were no young men left to take care of agricultural and household activities. This created a huge labour shortage and agricultural activities were affected most. Many of the women had to take extra burden of work when their husbands left their homes. They had to take dual responsibilities of household chores and agricultural activities including crop production, livestock, horticulture, marketing of agricultural products.[6]

In certain villages, the women had even to burn the dead bodies and they had to plough the agricultural land as there were no male members to perform such activities. Those were some of the activities that the women were forbidden to do by tradition. Besides, they had to deal with the security forces and the insurgents. There were several cases of the women and girls being victimised by the warring factions. Cases of rapes and violations of human rights were common.

---

[5] B.C. Upreti, *Maoists in Nepal: From Insurgency to Political Mainstream.* (New Delhi: Kalpaz Publications), pp. 192-93.

[6] Bishnu Raj Upreti, *Armed Conflict and Peace Process in Nepal: The Maoist insurgency, past negotiations, and opportunities for conflict transformation.* (New Delhi: Adroit Publishers,2010) pp. 273-74.

Many women were even forced to make their living through prostitution, particularly in towns. Those who lived in the villages deliberately allowed their daughters to move to the towns and cities so that they could escape the atrocities perpetrated by the warring forces. Many of those girls aged between 15 and 30 years were compelled to make earnings by working at the restaurants as dancers, waitresses as cabin girls and indulging in immoral practices in major towns of Nepal. Estimates are that the number of such girls numbered 70,000 in different districts of Nepal.[7]

After the Maoists consolidated their position, they began to collect taxes in various parts of Nepal. As the government was paralyzed, parallel bodies were formed by the Maoists to levy tax. In several pockets of the country, the vehicles were forced to pay road tax to the Maoists. Besides, the Maoists extorted money from several government officials, school teachers, business communities, industrialists and other groups of people. They imposed tax on the transit points such as at Pancheshwar, Dimber, Baker and Dharmaghat in Baitdi district.[8]They also collected tax from the persons dealing with trade in *Yarchagumba* (medicinal herb) in the high Himalayas. All such activities helped the Maoist party to raise huge amount of money, but this also made negative impact in government's efforts to mobilise resources from the public.

Besides, the Maoist party confiscated the private properties of a large number of people during the conflict period. There are reports that the Maoists confiscated 12,000 pieces of properties,[9] which they are unwilling to return to the rightful owners. Even they damaged the private properties of several individuals both in the rural and urban areas. This was not only a loss to the individuals concerned, but it was also a loss of the state. Many of the politicians claimed several times more compensation against the loss of their property than their actual valuation, which greatly strained the treasury of the national exchequer.

---

[7] Bishnu P. Poudel and Hari Bansh Jha, No. 5, p. 61.

[8] Bishnu Raj Upreti, no. 7, p. 260.

[9] Ramesh Khatry, "Looters' republic," My Republica, 25 March 2012 in http://www.myrepublica.com/portal/index.php?action=news_details&news_id=33178

Economic Impacts

Much of the regular economic activities were reduced, if not stopped, during the conflict period in Nepal. Funds were largely diverted to activities aimed at fighting against the Maoists. There was hardly any sector of the economy that was not affected during the conflict period – be it agriculture, industry, employment and livelihood and foreign aid. An account of the loss to some of those sectors is given below.

Decline in GDP and Investment

The GDP of the country declined and turned to be lowest (0.8 per cent) in 2001-2002.[10] Statistics show that Nepal's GDP was 4.8 per cent between 1990 and 2000, which declined drastically to 2.6 per cent between 2001 and 2005. On an average, there was a loss of 2.6 per cent in GDP annually after 2001.[11] Private investment rate declined from 15.4 per cent to 12.6 per cent between 1996 and 2004. The rate of economic growth in the country did not exceed 3.5 per cent until 2011-12, which is almost lowest in South Asia.

Growing Expenditure on Security

The development expenditures of government plummeted from 9 per cent of the GDP in 2001 to 6 per cent in 2004.[12] Much of the resources of the state in the conflict years were spent on combating the rebel forces. Between 2001 and 2004, expenditure on security almost doubled from 1.6 per cent of the GDP to 3 per cent of the GDP.[13] Military purchases during that period increased phenomenally. Estimates are that nearly 20 per cent of the budget amounting to $1.8 billion was diverted to the security sector in 2005-06. The defence budget in the country was tripled from Rs. 4 billion to Rs. 12 billion a year between 1996 and 2006. One of the factors that were responsible for the growth in security sector budget was the increase

---

[10] B.C. Upreti, no. 6.

[11] Bishnu Raj Upreti, no. 7, p. 257.

[12] Frances Stewart, "How Does Conflict Undermine Human Development?" in http://hdrstatsnet.undp.org/forum/messageview.cfm?catid=12&threadid=141

[13] Bishnu P. Poudel and Hari Bansh Jha, no. 5, p. 27.

in the number of Nepalese Army from 46,000 to 96,000 during the period between 1996 and 2006.[14]

Moreover, the Maoist party also spent quite a huge amount of money to keep the insurgency movement going. Statistics show that their operation cost amounted to nearly 15 million rupees each day during the conflict period over and above the cost involved in buying the weapons.[15] Interestingly, the Maoist army constituted 30-35 per cent of the women.[16]

Even after the signing of the Comprehensive Peace Agreement in 2006, a colossal amount of money was spent by the government of Nepal on 19,500 Maoist combatants, who stayed at seven major and 21 satellite camps in different parts of Nepal. In 2009-10, the government had to spend two billion rupees on the salary, ration and management of the Maoist combatants. Over and above a *per diem* amounting to Rs. 72 to Rs. 110, the combatants were paid Rs. 5,000.00 as monthly salary. In 2009-10, the government spent Rs. 570 million for the upgradation of infrastructure in the surrounding of the camps.[17]

Squeezing of Banking and Small Financial Institutions

During the conflict period, the Maoists had targeted the banking and financial institutions, particularly the state-owned banks. A number of banks in different parts of the country were looted and robbed.[18] This compelled the banks, particularly the commercial banks and Agricultural Development Bank to withdraw from the remote and rural areas and confine their activities mostly to the safer places like in the district headquarters. The banking and financial institutions were severely affected because of the lack of prospect of investment and also due to the market disruption, uncertainties and insecurity

---

[14] Kul Chandra Gautam, "Rollback violence," Nepali Times, July 17, 2009 in http://www.nepalitimes.com.np/issue/2009/07/17/GuestColumn/16127.

[15] Bishnu Raj Upreti. no. 7, p. 255.

[16] Ibid, pp. 272-73..

[17] http://www.nepalnews.com/main/index.php/news-archive/19-general/9317-almost-two-billion-spent-for-maoist-combatants-in-a-year.html

[18] Armin Hofmann and Helmut Grossmann. *Rural Finance in Conflict Environments - Experiences from Nepal's Small-Farmer Cooperatives Limited.* (Kathmandu: GTZ,2005) p. 6.

prevailing in the economy.

Even the micro financial institutions and Small Farmer Co-operative Limited were not spared during the conflict period. The Maoists forced them to reduce interest rates. They also encouraged the clients of such financial bodies to stop paying back loans. But at the same time the Savings and Credit Cooperatives, informal savings and credit groups and women-managed Small Farmer Co-operative Limited were spared. Perhaps, this was due to the reason that they were non-government and non-profit making bodies.[19] Nevertheless, the income and other opportunities of the stakeholders of those institutions were greatly affected due to the curb in movement of the people, and extortion of taxes from the people and local organizations.[20]

Migration of Productive Labour Force

A sizeable chunk of the Nepalese youth fled to different countries of the world, including in India, the Gulf countries and the Middle East. The number of people escaping to India in search of livelihood and their own security increased unprecedentedly. Nearly 24,000 people belonging to 3,500 households of Rajapur areas of Bardiya district in Nepal left their village enemas and migrated to Baharaich and Bachya areas across the border in India.

Estimates are that the number of people crossing over the Nepal-India border to India increased up to 2,000 per day.[21] In November-December 2002, the number of people crossing over to India from Nepalgunj sector varied from 300 to 400 each day; whereas the figures of such people crossing over to India during the same period in 2003 averaged to be 1,200.[22] Estimates are that nearly 2 million people fled to overseas countries for employment during the conflict period; while millions of people crossed over to India for similar purpose during that period.

---

[19] Ibid.

[20] Ibid.

[21] www.ipsnews.co.th/writingpeace/features/nepal.html

[22] Save the Children - Norway. " A Study of Impacts of Armed Conflict Pushing Girls and Women into Sexual Abuse and Sex Trade" *Kathmandu*, 2005.

Due to the surge in the migration of population from Nepal to foreign countries, the inflow of remittance recorded massive increase. Remittance constituted only 2.03 per cent of the GDP in 2000, which increased to 14.9 per cent in 2005, 22.09 per cent in 2010.[23]

In 2001, the volume of remittances from the overseas workers was US $139 million, which increased to US $808 million in 2004.[24] The remittance further increased from US $900 million in 2005 to US$2.7 billion in 2009.[25]

The remittance has made significant contribution to the economy of Nepal.[26] It helped the country avert devastating financial crisis caused by shrinking productivity and competitiveness. It helped the country to withstanding unfavorable balance of payments situation. It averted the crisis in foreign exchange reserve position. It was mainly on account of remittance that the poverty level in the country declined from 42 per cent to 31 per cent between 1996 and 2005 and further to 25.4 per cent in 2009.[27]

Information given by the Department of Foreign Employment suggest that over 1,500 Nepalese are leaving the country daily for employment in overseas countries. Former member of National Planning Commission Ganesh Gurung stated, "Hiring of Nepali workers, particularly unskilled labor, is increasing as Nepali laborers are cheaper and more honest compared to workers from other countries."[28] Estimates are that the remittance inflows will continue to grow at 10-12 per cent annually in the years to come.

---

[23] Anjan Pandey and Prakash Kumar Shrestha, "Parasitical State: Economic Consequences of Remittance," in Nepalnews.com, February 14, 2012 in http://www.nepalnews.com/home/index.php/top-column-hidden-menu/16659-parasitical-st

[24] Armin Hofmann and Helmut Grossmann, no. 19, p. 3.

[25] The World Bank. *Nepal Economic Update* 2010, p 15.

[26] My Republica, June 30, 2011.

[27] THT Online, "Nepal seeks global support to eradicate poverty" in the Himalayan Times, February 7, 2012 in http://www.thehimalayantimes.com/fullNews.php? headline=%27Nepal+seeks+global+supp....

[28] The Kathmandu Post, June 20, 2011.

Displacement of Population

The Inter-Agency Internal Displacement Division Mission to Nepal (11-22 April 2005) in its report found that nearly 200,000 people were internally displaced on account of the conflict; while those who moved to India during those years numbered 2 million.[29] Some of the factors that led to displacement of population included security risks at home from the warring factions, killing and torture of family members and religious persecution. The displacement of the population to comparatively safer places like the district headquarters, towns, road sides and the capital city in Kathmandu increased pressure on the existing basic infrastructure like the roads, water supplies, sanitation, water management and housing, and rise in the price of land. [30]

As per the government estimate, the number of people displaced formed 5,656 only; while UNDP estimated the figure somewhere between 150,000 and 200,000 and the Force Nepal came out with the figure of 400,000. [31] There have also been estimates of 600,000 people getting internally displaced in the country during the conflict period.

Decline in Agricultural Sector

Agriculture sector alone provides employment opportunities to over 80 per cent of the population in the country.[32] However, this sector met major jolt during the conflict period as the extension and outreach services, input supply and marketing networks were all disrupted. Besides, the traditional production relations in several parts of the country were disturbed by the Maoist slogan of 'land to the tillers'. They encouraged the tenants, poor farmers and marginalized people to grab such land. They asked the tenants not to pay contractual payments to the landlords. Instead, they wanted that the crop intended to be given to the landlords be handed over to them. On account of some of those factors, the farmers' interest in the land declined all the time

---

[29] Bishnu Raj Upreti, no 7, p. 251.

[30] Ibid, p. 252-53.

[31] *Annpurn Post*, July 7 & 29, 2005.

[32] Practical Action Nepal, "Minimising impacts of conflict," in http://practicalaction.org/impacts-of-conflict-1

low. Many farmers even left the agricultural land uncultivated rather than giving it to the tenants for farming out of the fear to loosing the land. There were cases of Maoist party making control over the big landholdings in certain parts of Nepal.[33] Even the rich commercial farmers who grew tea in Ilam and Panchathr were asked to pay hefty amount to the Maoist party.

As a result of haphazard approaches, there was negative effect on the production and productivity of agricultural land. Production of tea, fruit, vegetables, livestock, cardamom, ginger and broom grass declined substantially. Investment in agricultural sector declined all the time low due to the growing uncertainties in agricultural activities. Investment in agricultural sector declined to as low as 1 per cent.[34] The Agricultural Development Bank lost its interest in making investment in the agricultural sector because its staffs were frequently targeted.[35] This affected the livelihood of bulk of the Nepalese poor people who depend heavily on agriculture.

During the conflict, the local *haat bazars* were also disrupted. There was shortage of essential goods and services in the country. Many of the farmers were compelled to throw their agricultural products such as milk and vegetables on the roads as it was not possible to transport them to the market during the time of strikes and *bandhs*. So many farmers turned to be bankrupt as a result of such activities.

Fall in Industrial Activities

It was during the conflict period that labour militancy grew most in all the industrial units in Nepal. This often resulted in closure of the units, halting of the production and raising the wages of the workers. Figures are that almost 20 to 25 per cent of the private sector sales in the rural market declined during the conflict period. Following the Royal Coup of February

---

[33] Bishnu Raj Upreti, No. 7, p. 280.

[34] Hari Bansh Jha. *A Rapid Situation Assessment on Agriculture and Migration in Nepal.* (Unpublished Report). Centre for Economic and Technical Studies, Kathmandu:2010, p. 27.

[35] Bishnu Raj Upreti, No. 7, pp. 280-81.

1, 2005, the rate of growth of local production of goods and services declined to as low as 2 per cent or so, which was in fact even lower than the rate of growth of population of the country.

Industrial production fell drastically as the production of carpet, garment, textile, tobacco, beverage, etc. declined, which reduced the export trade of the country. Besides, the trade and commerce was affected due to the harassment to the business persons, industrialists and local shopkeepers. A number of the investors were forced to stop their activities as most of their staff living in the rural areas was threatened.[36]

Erosion of Joint Venture Projects

The rate of private investment declined from 15.4 per cent in 1996 to 12.6 per cent in 2004. Amidst frequent strikes, blockades, shutdowns and extortion demands, the foreign investors refrained from making any investment in Nepal.[37] Many of the Indian joint ventures were also targeted during the period. No new joint ventures have entered from India to Nepal for last several years. Most significantly, none of the Indian joint ventures operating in Nepal feel secure – be it Dabur Nepal, Surya Nepal, GMR working on Upper Karnali and Upper Marshyangdi or the United Telecom Limited (UTL). In view of this reality, S. M. Krishna, former India's External Affairs Minister wanted Nepal government to provide due protection to the Indian joint ventures in the country, whose contribution in terms of providing capital and employment opportunities is significant.[38]

The conflict had a negative impact on the multinational companies working in Nepal. For example, Colgate Palmolive Nepal P. Limited had to close its operations in Hetauda partly due to Nepal government's failure to comply with its commitment to exemption of income tax and partly due to the insecurity, strikes and *bandhs*.[39] There were frequent cases of burning

---

[36] B.C. Upreti, No. 6, p. 193.

[37] Sungsup Ra and Bipul Singh. "Nepal: Measuring the Economic Costs of Conflict: The Effect of Declining Development Expenditure" in Asian Development Bank: Working Paper Series No. 2. Nepal Resident Mission, 2005

[38] Hari Bansh Jha, "SM Krishna's visit to Nepal," My Republica, April 25, 2011 in http://myrepublica.com/portal/index.php?action=news-details&news-id=30609

[39] Bishnu Raj Upreti, no. 7, pp. 252-53.

of the industries. Jyoti Spinning Mills in Sarlahi was burnt. Because of the closure of the industries, many of the workers lost their source of livelihood. Other noted companies such as Uniliver Nepal, Surya Tobacco Company, Coca-Cola Company, distilleries, etc. were frequently targeted. Some big hotels were compelled to close on account of labour militancy. Even big business companies in the private sector were asked to pay hefty donations.

Dwindling Foreign Aid

The Royal Coup of February 1, 2005 annoyed the donor agencies most. As such, they suspended or postponed an estimated $250 million worth of development aid to Nepal. This affected many of the programmes aimed at poverty reduction, rural development, education, health and forestry.[40] Norway cancelled its investment programme worth Rs. $500 million; whereas the World Bank withdrew US$65 million investment programme. It was feared if Nepal could be declared a failed state as the donor countries were apprehensive of Nepal government's attempt to ensure implementation of donor-supported projects. Such countries as Japan, Switzerland, Canada, Finland, England, Germany, Norway, Denmark, EU and the Netherlands even suspended their aid programmes in the Maoist affected areas, particularly in the mid and far western region of Nepal.[41]

Damage and Destruction of Infrastructural Facilities

During the conflict, many of the infrastructural facilities, including police posts, health posts, roads, government offices, airports, jails, radio stations, bridges, Village Development Committees, Municipalities and schools were either destructed or damaged, which coasted heavily to the national exchequer.

---

[40] Surendra R. Devkota, "Politico-Economics of Royal Takeover in Nepal" in www.globalpolitician.com/21134-economics.

[41] Gunanidhi Sharma, "Cost of Conflict and Donors' Dilemma: How is Nepal Coping?" in Ananda P Shrestha and Hari Upreti (Ed.). *Critical Barriers to the Negotiation of Armed Conflict in Nepal.* Kathmandu: Nepal Foundation for Advanced Studies,2004, p. 161.

Electricity

The situation in power sector worsened when the Maoists targeted power stations in different parts of the country. In the post-conflict era, not much effort was made to enhance power. Therefore, there is a huge load shedding problem in the country. Many parts of the country are plunged in darkness as the existing supply of power of 600 MW does not meet the demand for electricity. Many of the industrial, agricultural and other sectors of the economy have been affected on account of the inadequate supply of electricity. In order to cope with the growing demand for power, the Nepalese government has been requesting the Indian government to provide power.

Sadly though, the Water Resources Committee of the Maoists in the past issued diktat to stop any further work on fourteen hydro projects under joint ventures mainly with Indian companies.[42] This diktat affected the work on Upper Karnali and Arun 3 projects. Significantly, survey license for those projects were awarded to two Indian multinational companies on the global competition bidding. The Indian companies had offered attractive package in the form of certain free energy. Such a move is expected to increase Nepal's dependence on India in power sector, which might lead to further outflow of foreign exchange and widening of balance of trade with India. Besides, it might further push the country towards backwardness.

In the past, the Maoists had opposed all major deals with India in water resource sector, including in the 6,000 MW Mahakali Treaty that was endorsed by the Nepalese Parliament by more than two-thirds majority in 1996. This four billion dollar project has not been materialized until today. The Maoists are not alone to be blamed for the non-implementation of the project, but then their opposition to the project certainly made a difference. A faction of the Maoists have opposed 10-point joint statement issued after the ministerial-level talks on water resources between Nepal and India held in New Delhi on February 15, 2012 in which the two countries had

---

[42] Ram S Mahat, "West Seti and Hydro Politics," My Republica, March 30, 2012 in http://www.myrepublica.com/portal/index.php?action=news_details&news_id=33356.

agreed to form Pancheshwar Development Authority, prepare detailed project report (DPR) for Koshi High Dam and construction of east-west dams for flood control across the Nepal-India border.[43] Besides, the faction also opposed the government decision to provide land to GMR Company on lease for the development of Upper Karnali Project.

Education System

During the conflict period, nearly 3,000 teachers had to give up teaching, which directly affected 100,000 school-going children in various parts of the country. Besides, 700 schools in the country were closed. Frequent *bandhs* and protests affected the education system most. This led many of the school-going children to discontinue their education. Many of the children were also used in the war as human shields, porters, housekeepers, cooks and in certain cases as sex slaves.[44]

Certain schools and other academic institutions were targeted both by the Maoists and the security forces during the conflict. They were grossly misused because their compounds were used as forts by the warring factions.

Future of thousands of children was affected with the introduction of commune, red education and recruitment of child soldiers in Maoist fighting cadets.[45] After the signing of Comprehensive Peace Agreement in 2006, all the major political parties in Nepal agreed to declare education institutions as protest-free zone. But even after six years of the signing of the Agreement, the education institutions are yet to be free from such protests. Quite often, the student unions shut down the education institutions on one or the other excuse. Sometimes, even the teachers forcefully closed schools throughout the country to get their demands fulfilled by the government.[46]

---

[44] Tek Raj Gyawali, "Socio-Economic Impact of Political Insurgency in Nepal," in http://management.kochi-tech.ac.jp/pdf/ssms200

[45] Ramesh Khatry, "Against the Tide It's only words," My Republica, February 26, 2012.

[46] Editorial, "Cool it guys," My Republica, February 28, 2012.

Tourism

The tourism sector occupies important place in the Nepalese economy as its share in GDP is 2 per cent. It also accounts for 12 per cent of the annual foreign currency earnings. But this sector was affected partly due to the fact that a negative publicity was given by different sources that Nepal was insecure and risky to travel. The USA and European countries had frequently warned their people to avoid traveling to Nepal due to the deterioration in law and order situation in the country.[47] Besides, there were several cases of Maoists forcing the tourists to pay donation and levy especially in the Maoist influenced area.[48] This led to gradual decline in the number of tourists visiting Nepal, which largely affected the growth of tourism industry in Nepal

Forest

There was a huge destruction of forest and its resources during the conflict period in Nepal. The Maoists had made the forest as their refuge. While they lived there, they fell trees on a large scale. As the forests were hiding place for many of the Maoists, the security forces burnt forests at several places. Taking undue advantage of the situation, much of the forest resources like medicinal plants, non-timber forest products and wild animals were smuggled. In addition, poaching and hunting of wild animals were rampant. Flora and fauna of forest were greatly destroyed. There was over harvesting of *Yarsagumba*, the high value medicinal plants. [49]

Cost of Damaging Infrastructure

The following table presents an account of the number of infrastructural facilities, including police posts, roads, forest, health damaged by the Maoists between February 1996 and July 2005. A brief account of the damages inflicted to the different infrastructures in the country is presented in the table below:

---

[47] Bharat Pokharel, "Comments" in Ananda P Shrestha and Hari Upreti (Ed.). *Critical Barriers to the Negotiation of Armed Conflict in Nepal.* Kathmandu: Nepal Foundation for Advanced Studies, p. 166.

[48] Bishnu Raj Upreti. No. 7, 2004 pp. 252-53.

[49] Ibid., p. 271.

Table 1: Infrastructures damaged by Maoists between February 1996 and July 2005.

Types of Infrastructures	Number
1. Police posts	579
2. District Police Offices	35
3. Post offices	641
4. Health posts	85
5. Roads	45
6. Forest office and range posts	290
7. Irrigation infrastructures	30
8. District Education Offices	34
9. Agricultural offices	149
10. Land Revenue offices	43
11. Land Reform offices	9
12. Soil conservation offices	8
13. Livestock offices	24
14. Women development offices	18
15. Revenue offices/units	22
16. Airports	14
17. Jails	7
18. Courts	18
19. Radio stations	2
20. National parks and reserves	8
21. Bridges	44
22. Dairy development units	9
23. Municipalities and wards	77

24. Village Development Committees	1621
25. Drinking water systems	22
26. Telecom towers	128
27. Powerhouses and electricity offices	96
28. Sajha transport	7
29. Food depots/stores	25
30. Schools	159
31. Treasury offices	5
32. Financial Institutions	222
33. Land measurement offices	15
34. Family planning offices/units	38
35. Others	619
Total	**5138**

Source: Samaya Weekly, Vol.2, No 69, 28/4-2/5 2062 (12-18 August 2005) p. 38 quoted from Bishnu Raj Upreti. 2010. Armed Conflict and Peace Process in Nepal: The Maoist insurgency, past negotiations, and opportunities for conflict transformation. New Delhi: Adroit Publishers, pp. 277-78.

Destruction of Infrastructural Network

Development activities in the Village Development Committees and District Development Committees came to a halt as the resources meant for their development were diverted to other sectors. There are reports that the buildings of about 1,500 Village Development Committees were partially or completely destroyed in different districts of the country.[50]

In the infrastructural sector, several telecommunication towers, roads, air strips, bridges, government buildings, banks, police stations, school buildings and power plants were damaged, which cost the nation $250 million

---

[50] Prakash S. Mahat, "Socio-economic Transformation of Rural Areas for Peace and Democracy," *The Telegraph Weekly*, July 5, 2006.

until 2002. The government property worth five billion rupees was destructed during that period.[51]

Cost of Conflict

The Federation of Nepalese Chambers of Commerce and Industry estimated the loss due to the bandhs ranging from Rs. 1.2 billion to Rs. 1.5 billion per day. Industrial strike affected the local production; while the transportation strikes and blockades paralyzed the entire economic activities in the region. The Private and Boarding School Organization of Nepal estimated the loss due to the educational strikes to the tune of Rs. 35 million per day.[52]

Estimates made by DFID shows that the decade-long conflict in Nepal coasted the nation 8-10 per cent of the GDP. On the other hand, the National Peace Campaign estimated the cost of conflict to the level of $66.2 billion between 1996 and 2003.[53] In some quarters, the economic cost of conflict was estimated at $2 billion.[54] The Asian Development Bank estimated that infrastructures worth $250 million was destroyed during the conflict period. The cost of reconstruction of the damaged infrastructure was recorded at $400 million; while the total cost of destruction of the physical infrastructure and development projects was to the tune of US $250 million.[55]

Interestingly, Table 2 presents an estimate of loss caused by conflict during 2001-02 and 2002-03. The government's expenditure on security during that period amounted to Rs. 39.63 billion against the Maoist Army's expense varying from Rs. 1.94 billion to Rs. 2.13 billion. Loss of physical infrastructures and banks during the period amounted to Rs. 25 billion. Similarly, the loss of income on account of damage to human resources amounted to 14.04 billion; whereas the loss due to shift of development expenditure amounted to 12.30 billion. The loss due to decrease in the number of tourists inflow was Rs. 11.05 billion; while the loss in income due

---

[51] Gunanidhi Sharma, No. 42, p. 155.

[52] Bharat Pokharel, No. 48, p. 167.

[53] Sungsup Ra and Bipul Singh. no. 38.

[54] Dev Raj Dahal. *Civil Society Groups in Nepal: Their Roles in Conflict and Peace Building.* (Kathmandu: Support for Peace and Development Initiative (UNDP),2005), p. 27.

[55] Bharat Pokharel, no. 48, p. 164.

to displacement was Rs. 8.00 billion, the loss of direct foreign investment was 6.05 billion, and the loss in business due to the strike and *bandhs* was 1.0 billion.

Table 2: Estimated cost of conflict in Nepal (2001-02 and 2002-03)

Expenditures/Loss	Cost (In billion rupees)
Direct Cost	
Direct expenditure on security (Govt)	39.63 (10% of GDP)
Maoist Army's Expense	1.94 - 2.13
Damage to physical infrastructures and banks	25.00
Sub-total	**66.63**
Indirect Cost	
Loss in business due to strike and Bandh (closure)	1.00
Loss due to decrease in the number of tourists inflow	11.05
Loss of income due to damage in human resources	14.04
Loss in income due to displacement	8.00
Loss due to shift of development expenditure for defence	12.30
Loss of the direct foreign investment	6.05
Sub-total	**52.44**
Total	**119.07**

Source: Rana and Sharma (2004) & Kumar (2004) in Bishnu Raj Upreti. 2010. Armed Conflict and Peace Process in Nepal: The Maoist insurgency, past negotiations, and opportunities for conflict transformation. New Delhi: Adroit Publishers, p. 258.

Confiscation of Land from the Owners

The land transactions were carried out by the Maoists during the conflict period in Maoist-controlled areas of Rolpa, Rukum, Salyan and Jajarkot at the initiative of Baburam Bhattrai, who was then a rebel leader and now the Prime Minister of Nepal. Such transactions were carried out by the Maoist party as parallel body of the government. Available information shows that there were 10,000 cases of land transactions in 10 Maoist-affected districts, included in Palpa, Gulmi, Baglung, Parbat, Arghakhanchi, Pyuthan, Rolpa, Salyan and Rukum. In Rukum district alone, there were around 4,000 cases of land deals during the conflict period.

The Maoists used to charge two per cent of the tax on each transaction done during the time of conflict. However, the land deals done during the time of insurgency has lost its legal entity now. Aarambikram Shah, Chief of Rukum District Revenue Office clearly said, "The legal body to register and pass land is a government body. All the land registered at agencies other than lawful government body is illegal." With the end of insurgency in the country, the rightful owners who sold their land during the time of insurgency are now reclaiming their land as the transaction of deals with People's government has lost its legal entity.[56]

In a major development, the government of Nepal made a decision on January 12, 2012 to legitimize the land transactions that were done by the Maoists during the conflict era. However, a writ petition was filed in Nepal's Supreme Court in which the petitioners sought intervention from the apex court against the Cabinet decision passed on January 12, 2012 to legalize the transaction of properties as the decision was against the provision of Interim Constitution and the existing laws of Nepal.[57] Accordingly, the Supreme Court issued a stay order on January 19, 2012.[58]

---

[56] Aadarsha KC, "War-era land deals number in thousands," The Himalayan Times, Februray 10, 2012.

[57] Himalayan News Service, "Land Office's authority encroached," *The Himalayan Times*, January 27, 2012.

[58] Himalayan News Service, "House moves ahead after govt backtracks," *The Himalayan Times*, February 10, 2012 in http://www.thehimalayantimes.com/fullTodays.php?headline =House+moves+ahead++afte....

The Deputy Attorney General Pushpa Raj Koirala defended the government stand on the legalization of transaction of properties on the ground that it did not violate the rights of the common people and the constitution. But a number of advocates pleading the case from the side of the petitioner found that the effort to legalize the transaction of properties was not only against the established principle of justice but also against the provision of the Nepalese constitution.

In addition, the Nepali Congress (NC) and CPN-UML obstructed the proceedings of Nepalese parliament from January 17, 2012 in their bid to pressurize the government of Nepal to withdraw the decision to legitimize land transactions carried out by the Maoists during the time of conflict in Nepal (1996-2006).[59] Several lawmakers in the Constituent Assembly charged that such a decision not only derailed the peace process, but it also affected the statute-drafting process. Arjun Narsingh KC of NC categorically said that the Maoist-led government would not last long if the decision to legalize the transaction of properties was not revoked.[60] On the other hand, 16 sister wings of UCPN (M) raised voice in favour of government's decision to legitimize the land transaction deal. Gunraj Lohani, Chief of the Maoist aligned All Nepal Teachers' Association said, "It is anti-people move and political dishonesty on the part of the parliamentary parties to oppose implementation of the cabinet decision. The peace agreements signed in the past have already acknowledged the dual governments during the conflict era."[61]

On January 26, 2012, the UCPN (M) decided that the government should not withdraw its decision to legalize the wartime transaction of

---

[59] Himalayan News Service, "Conflict-era land transactions keep House on the boil," *The Himalayan Times*, January 27, 2012.

[60] Nepalnews.com, "NC to bring down govt if controversial decision to legalise war-era land deals nto scraped," January 30, 2012 in http://www.nepalnews.com/archive/2012/jan/jan30/news02.php

[61] Republica, "Maoist wings want land deal decision implemented,: *My Republica*, January 30, 2012 in http://www.myrepublica.com/portal/index.php?action=news_details&news_id=41421

properties.[62] But in view of the mounting pressure from the opposition political parties, the government of Nepal declared that it would not implement the controversial decision to recognize wartime land and property dealings.

Economic and Fiscal Changes for Resolving Conflict

There was a lack of political commitment on the part of the leaders and government to increase investment and generate employment opportunities by giving vigorous drive to development activities. Instead of pumping its resources in investment in infrastructure sectors like in education, health, roads, rails, airports and power, the government diverted most of its resources to the security sector. The government had also little concern for safeguarding the production in industrial and agricultural sectors, which generated massive employment opportunities in the country. Vocational education and skill development programmes were overlooked. Human capital formation was ignored as many of the educational institutions had virtually turned into forts by the warring factions. It is likely that some of those measures could have helped the government resolve the conflict, but not much effort was made in this direction.

Present Political Arrangement and Conflict

In 2011-12, the Relief and Rehabilitation Division under the Ministry of Peace and Reconstruction had released Rs. 1.79 billion for distribution among the families of those killed, Rs. 199.8 million for families of the disappeared and Rs. 124.5 million for the wives of the disappeared.[63] Because a large number of people were displaced and migrated elsewhere for security reasons and in search of livelihood during the conflict period, there were cases in which certain rightful claimants did not turn up to receive relief package offered to them by the government. Some 3,864 families of the 17,883 persons killed during the Maoist insurgency could

---

[62] Republica, "Govt decision strains parties-Maoist relations further," My Republica, January 27, 2012 in http://www.myrepublica.com/portal/index.php?action=news_details&news _id=41308.

[63] Gani Ansari, "Victims' non-acceptance of relief package worries govt," My Republica March 14, 2012 in http://www.myrepublica.com/portal/index.php?action=news_ details&news_id=32792.

not turn for such support. Since 2008, the government has been providing Rs. 100,000 each to the families of people killed during the conflict. Wives of persons killed were offered additional Rs. 25,000 by the government.

Because of political fragile situation, there has been mushroom growth in the crime rates in the country. Many criminal armed groups have been set up. They indulge in numerous criminal activities, which have led to the growth of big business in illegally manufactured home made arms, particularly in the Terai/Madehsh and Kathmandu Valley. [64] Estimates are that the armed groups, criminals, private militia and common people possessed about 55,000 small arms and light weapons.[65] With the criminalization of the society, the cases of murder, rape, drug trafficking, smuggling, trafficking in women, vulgarism and hooliganism, looting and kidnapping have increased over the years.[66] Due to the presence of so many armed groups in the Terai region, it is difficult for many people to travel from one part of the country to the other.

However, in the recent past some breakthrough has been made towards rehabilitating the Maoist combatants. Understanding is also developed among the major political parties of Nepal to integrate certain combatants in the Nepalese army. Yet some hurdles exist in resolving the problem as mentioned below:

Mishandling in Voluntary Retirement Scheme

In 2006, the Nepalese government had established 28 cantonment sites in the country to accommodate the Maoist combatants. Accordingly, the People's Liberation Army (PLA) was put in different cantonments in Nepal in 2007. The government of Nepal gave the Maoist combatants the choice of voluntary retirement in 2012. Accordingly, those combatants who chose to retire voluntarily were given incentives varying between Rs. 500,000

---

[64] Chuda Bahadur Shrestha, "Crime Prevention, Ensuring Public Safety and Nepal Police," in *Nepal's National Interests:Foreign Policy, Internal Security, Federalism, Ene3rgy-Economy*. 2011. Tomislav Delinic and Nischal N. Pandey (Ed.), Kathmandu: Centre for South Asian Studies and Konard Adenauer Stiftung, p. 260.

[65] Kul Chandra Gautam, no. 15.

[66] Bishnu Raj Upreti, no. 7, p. 250.

and 800,000. [67] In the first installment, each of the 7,365 combatants who opted for voluntary retirement was given an amount of Rs. 250,000 to Rs. 400,000.

But at the time the PLA combatants were provided cheques against voluntary retirement, they were forced by the commanders to share part of the amount. Those who dared to defy the command were dealt with harshly. However, some efforts were made to pacify the disgruntled combatants on the ground that the Maoist party would use the money collected from the combatants to provide relief packages to the disqualified and minors already discharged some two years ago.

A number of combatants in several camps complained that their combatants indulged in snatching their pay cheques and identity cards. About 30 combatants formally complained to the Special Committee (for supervision, integration and rehabilitation of Maoist fighters) Secretariat about the commanders who forced them to share certain percent of their voluntary retirement package through such act as seizing their paychecks or withholding their identity cards.[68] Identity cards are instrumental in the sense that it was needed to claim their retirement package and also to withdraw money from the banks to encash their paychecks.

The Special Committee took the development with regard to the snatching of the cheques to the Maoist combatants by their own commanders quite seriously. In fact, the commanders not only snatched the cheques of the fighters but they also forced them to sign blank cheques. So to ensure that only the retiring fighters opting for voluntary retirement receive money, the Special Committee directed the three government banks, including Nepal Bank Limited, Rastriya Banijya Bank and Agriculture Development Bank, to deposit money in the accounts of the concerned combatants only when they appeared to the concerned bank in person to encash the cheque. The

---

[67] Kamal Dev Bhattarai, "Maoist party to give cash incentives to YCL cadres," February 8, 2012 in http://www.ekantipur.com/2012/02/08/top-story/maoist-party-to-give-cash-incentives-to-ycl...

[68] Republica, "30 complaints at secretariat against commanders," in My Republica, February 10, 2012 in http://www.myrepublica.com/portal/index.php?action=news _details& news_id=41840...

banks were told that they would be made accountable in case anyone else received payment without the signature of the concerned fighter on the cheques.[69]

However, sources close to Maoist party revealed that the effort made by the commanders to snatch the cheques and to withhold the identity cards of the Maoist combatants was due to the assurance given by them to the party that they would provide 50 per cent of the money from their financial reward scheme to the party. There is report that many of the absentee combatants were recalled to the cantonments following the announcement by the government to provide voluntary retirement package to them.[70] Speculations are that the number of absentee combatants was much more than what it was found by the Special Committee surveyor team during the verification period in December 2011.

There were reports that Pushpa Kamal Dahal faction of the Maoists justified the effort to take certain portion of money from the retiring PLA combatants in order to pay for the relief to YCL members and the disqualified combatants. But the other faction led by Vice Chairman Mohan Baidya wanted that there should not be any cut on the incentives provided to the PLA combatants.

A number of disgruntled fighters in the first division in Ilam announced week-long protest programmes from February 12, 2012 against the Maoist Party's decision to pocket part of the retirement cash from them.[71] They demanded that the seized cheques and identity cards should be returned to them. Also, they wanted disqualified fighters and YCL members to be compensated from the PLA Fund. Most importantly, they threatened to defect the party *en mass* in case their demands were not met. Meanwhile, there were reports that many of the cheques that were seized by the

---

[69] Himalayan News Service, "Special panel to ask banks to put PLA cheques on hold," *The Himalayan Times*, February 10, 2012 in http://www.thehimalayantimes.com/fullNews.php?headline=Special+panel+to+ask+banks....

[70] Editorial, "Beleaguered UCPN (M)," My Republica, February 8, 2012 in http://www.myrepublica.com/portal/index.php?action=news_details&id=id=41788

[71] Chetan Adhikari and Mohan Budaair, "Now, retiring PLA 'moms' up in arms," *The Kathmandu Post*, February 12, 2012.

commanders were already cashed. Retired combatant Pradeep Kumar Shrestha said, "A new feudalism has started in the Maoist party with the cheque-grab. We gave ourselves to topple such feudalism once, but now are suffering at the hands of our own party men."[72]

Besides, as a mark of protest the YCL cadres seized the vehicle used by Maoist Politburo member. Former PLA and disabled combatants submitted memorandum to the Maoist Politburo member in Jajarkot district to provide them relief packages. In order to pacify the dissatisfied the YCL members, the Standing Committee meeting of the Maoist party decided to provide cash incentives to them. In addition, they decided to provide some relief packages to the disqualified and minor combatants who got discharged two years ago. The disqualified and minor combatants who were discharged were also up in arms for they wanted same facilities as given to PLA combatants, though they were provided vocational training by various NGOs supported by UNICEF Nepal office.

The Special Committee was able to complete its job of providing cheques to 7,200 former Maoist fighters out of the total 7,365 fighters who opted for voluntary retirement.[73] Those fighters who could not receive their cheques were asked to do so from the secretariat in Kathmandu. Thus, the process of discharging the 7,365 Maoist combatants opting for voluntary retirement was completed between February 2 and February 11, 2012.

Subsequently, the number of Maoist combatants seeking integration declined more than their allotted quota of 6,500 because additional 4,080 combatants took voluntary retirement and left the cantonments with their paychecks. With this development, 5,625 combatants are left in the cantonments. Expectations are that the number of combatants opting for integration with the Nepalese army would be only in the range of 3,000 to 5,000.[74]

---

[72] Himalayan News Service, "Combatants announce agitation against cheque snatching," *The Himalayan Times*, February 12, 2012.

[73] Nepalnews.com, "Distribution of cheque to retiring combatants complete,"February 12, 2012 in http://www.nepalnews.com/archive/2012/feb/feb12/news01.php.

[74] Kiran Pun, Integration number likely to be around 3,000," *My Republica*, April 15, 2012 in http://www.myrepublica.com/portal/index.php?action=news_details&news_id=33932

Misuse of PLA Fund

Estimates are that Rs. 3 billion was deposited in the PLA fund, which included Rs. 1.14 billion from the monthly salaries of each of the combatants, Rs. 1.34 billion drawn in the name of absentee combatants and Rs. 600 million as commissions against ration contracts.[75]

Each month the Maoist party deducted Rs. 1,000 from the salaries of the combatants ever since their verification was completed by United Nation Mission to Nepal in 2007.[76] The total amount of money generated by deducting Rs. 1,000 from each of the 19,525 combatants during last five years formed Rs. 1.14 billion, which was deposited in PLA fund.[77] The PLA fund was created with the promise that 50 per cent of the money would go to the YCL; while the remaining money would be returned to the combatants during their retirement time.[78]

The second source PLA fund amounting to Rs. 1.34 billion was collected from the salaries of the absentee combatants during last five years. As it is well known, the PLA received salary and ration allowance for the entire 19,525 combatants, though the surveyor teams of Special Committee in December 2011 found that 2,432 combatants were missing from the cantonments. As the government provided Rs. 9,230 to each combatant as their salary and ration, the total amount of money that the PLA commanders generated in the name of absentee combatants over the years formed Rs. 1.34 billion.

Finally, the third source of PLA fund came from commission given by the contractors to PLA. On average, each month the government provided Rs. 2,730 to each of the 19,525 combatants as ration allowance. It is believed

---

[75] Kiran Pun, "Combatants suspect misuse of Rs. 3 billion from PLA fund," My Republica, February 9, 2012 in http://www.myrepublica.com/portal/index.php?action= news_ details&news_id=41832

[76] Kamal Dev Bhattarai, "Pocketing fighters' cash party's policy" February 7, 2012 in http://www.ekantipur.com/2012/02/07/top-story/pocketing-fighters-cash-partys-policy/3485...

[77] Kiran Pun, No. 76.

[78] Kiran Pun, "Why the cantonments imploded?" My Republica, April 11, 2012.

that the total amount that the PLA could have generated from the contractors during five years as commission was Rs. 600 million.[79]

However, the PLA commanders revealed that they had only 460 million in total in PLA fund, when they were hard pressed by the combatants to become transparent about the money deposited in the fund.[80]

The Nepal Army has secured all the weapons lying in the containers in the presence of monitors. It is now in charge of camps, fighters and their weapons.[81] However, the Maoist hardliner faction led by Vice-chairman Mohan Baidya protested against this move to deploy Nepal Army in the People's Liberation Army cantonments by taking out a torch rally in Kathmandu.[82]

Unresolved YCL Issue

As per the media report, 3,500 PLA members have still been working for the YCL,[83] which is over and above those who either migrated abroad for employment or joined other political parties by severing their relations with the party. They had joined the YCL under the directive of the Maoist party. In fact, the YCL members were the hardcore Maoist fighters, who left the PLA and joined the YCL at the instruction of the Maoist leadership. The YCL was formed as a separate force presumably to work for the party in all possible ways. They lived in the camps at different urban locations as combatants.

The YCL demanded monetary repayment for their service in the party as they could not get anything from the government. They asked the party to provide them facilities in par with the PLA fighters. It was disclosed that the party had savings ranging from Rs. 180 million to Rs. 410 million,[84]

[79] Kiran Pun, No. 76.

[80] Ibid.

[81] Himalayan News Service, "Army secure PLA weapons" The Himalayan Times, April 12, 2012.

[82] Nepalnews, "Baidya faction takes out tourch rally" http://www.nepalnews.com/archive/2012/apr/apr11/news16.php on april 12, 2012.

[83] Republica, "PLA to disclose finances to YCL but demands reciprocity," My Republica, March 12, 2012.

[84] Kiran Pun, "No savings in PLA accounts: Commanders," My Republica, April 20, 2012.

which was too small amount to satisfy the YCL members. Expressing his frustration, Ashal Khadka, Vice-coordinator of YCL Magarat State Committee even said, "We attended the meeting not to beg for money but to demand transparency in the PLA fund."[85]

With the growing intra-party rift in UCPN (Maoist), the radical faction of the party led by Senior Vice-Chairman Mohan Baidya announced phase-wise programmes till May 28 with a view to toppling their own government. The protest programmes aim at creating pressure for providing relief packages and treatment to the injured and the kin of martyrs and the disappeared persons, addressing the reasonable demands of YCL, dignified PLA integration and framing a pro-people constitution.

The Maoist party is trapped in a controversy. The party would require minimum Rs. 2 billion to compensate the YCL cadres.[86] If the party pays this amount to the YCL, the Election Commission of Nepal might raise a question about the source of income of the party. Most importantly, the party in its report submitted to Election Commission had disclosed its annual income as half a billion rupees.

Future Direction

At a time Nepal needed stable and effective government to address different issues of conflict, political uncertainty has cropped up with the dissolution of 601-member Constituent Assembly (CA) on May 28, 2012. Despite its repeated extensions for four times, the CA failed to make the constitution during its total tenure of four years until May 27, 2012. As a result, even the position of Maoist-led government has become questionable. The President of the Nepal, Ram Baran Yadav treats the present Bhattarai-led government as care taker until the next government is formed; while the Prime Minister treats himself qualified to conduct the next elections of Parliament in Apr/ May 2013.

---

[85] Republica, "Leaders insulted us: YCL cadres," My Republica, March 17, 2012.

[86] Republica, Show me the money," My Republica, February 12, 2012.

Uncertainty created by the dissolution of CA would seriously affect the private sector, including the domestic and foreign investors. The entrepreneurs would find it difficult to safeguard their investments because of the lack of congenial climate in the country. Conflict and insecurity still dominate the political scene of the country. In the existing situation when there is political instability and law and order situation is deteriorating, the industrial sector is likely to meet a major set back. They would also be affected by the power shortage and growing labour militancy in the country. Many of the industries which were forced to operate below capacity would find it harder to survive. It is unlikely that the government would be able to procure Rs. 300 billion foreign investment in the year 2012-13, which is declared as Nepal Investment Year. Ultimately, all this would affect the employment prospects. In the existing situation, it is likely that many of the investors would like to move elsewhere, which would further erode the prospect of recovery in the country.

Amidst the gloomy economic scenario, the productive youth force in the country would continue to migrate abroad. This would affect the growth of development activities in the country. This is more so as the government has failed to spend even 50 per cent of the development budget allocated for the development projects.[87] The tourism sector is also likely to be affected in a situation that is plagued by political instability. All such developments show that the conflict is not likely to be addressed so easily in Nepal.

Conclusions

The Maoist insurgency gave a major jolt to the peaceful nation Nepal. It impacted almost all the sectors of the country. There was hardly any part of the country that was not affected. Though the conflict came to the end in 2006 with the signing of Comprehensive Peace Agreement, peace is not yet restored in the country. Over the years, there has been proliferation of small arms throughout the country, particularly in the Terai region of Nepal. Most of the armed groups created in the post-Maoist insurgency period are the splinter groups of the Maoists and they will pose law and order problem

---

[87] Editorial, "Bleak prospects" *The Himalayan Times*, May 30, 2012.

to the administration for a long time to come. The government has very little control over them. Much of the economic resources that could perhaps have been spent on development are still being diverted to the security sector and in maintaining law and order situation in the country.

However, there was one silver lining during the time of conflict. People fled the country in the same way as the bees sometimes leave the hives. With the eviction of people from Nepal to India and different overseas countries, there was huge upsurge in the remittance in the country. The country continued to reap the dividend of remittance even in the post-conflict period after 2006 as the flow of migrants from Nepal to foreign countries went on increasing. Remittance also played key role in reducing the number of population below the poverty lines over last few years.

Another major development in conflict mediation was addressing the issue of Maoist combatants living in different cantonments of the country. Quite sizeable sections of the Maoists have opted for voluntary retirement and others have been waiting for integration with the Nepalese army.

But what is worrying is that the Maoists lacked transparency in distributing PLA Funds. They were also open to criticism for snatching the cheque of the combatants who opted for voluntary retirement. The YCL structure is yet to be dismantled and the private property confiscated by the Maoists during the time of conflict is not yet returned to the rightful owners. The Truth and Reconciliation Commission and Commission of Disappeared People could not be formed. There has also been discontent and chaos in each part of the country with regard to evolving federal states. And on top of all this the CA was dissolved on May 27 for its failure to come out with the constitution. As a result, the present government has merely become caretaker till the next government is formed. In the present situation, the political roadmap of Nepal looks bumpy. If the political leaders do not show maturity, it is likely that the conflict would further flare up in different parts of the country on ethnic, regional and other grounds, which would have detrimental effect on development.

Contributors

Dr. Nishchal N. Pandey is Director of the Centre for South Asian Studies, Kathmandu and is a well known Nepali strategic analyst. He has authored, edited and coedited many books on the Nepali political and strategic issues. Dr. Pandey holds a Ph.D. from Tribhuvan University, Kathmandu and was visiting fellow at the Institute of South Asian Studies (ISAS), Singapore in 2006-07. He is at present international research committee member of the Regional Centre for Strategic Studies, Colombo and visiting fellow at the Institute of Peace and Conflict Studies, New Delhi. He was also Advisor to the National Planning Commission of Nepal.

Ambassador Jayant Prasad is a member of Indian Foreign Services and currently Indian Ambassador to Nepal. He has served as India's Permanent Representative to the Conference on Disarmament, Geneva, Ambassador to Algeria; Counsellor for trade access and development cooperation at the Indian Mission to the European Union in Brussels, First Secretary in the Permanent Mission of India to the United Nations, Geneva and Second Secretary in the Embassy of India in Paris.

Mr Gopal K Pillai is former Union Home Secretary. He was also Principal Secretary to the Chief Minister of Kerala Mr AK Antony, currently the Union Defence Minister. He has worked in the ministries of Defence, Shipping and Surface transport, Home Affairs and Commerce. He was actively involved in the WTO as India's Chief Negotiator. Post retirement, he is a distinguished Fellow in the Institute of Defence Studies and Analyses, Chairman of Ivy Cap Ventures Advisors Pvt Ltd, a venture capital fund promoted by the IIT Alumni Trust and is the RK Mishra Chair of the Observer Research Foundation.

Dr Lok Raj Baral is Professor and Executive Chairman of Nepal Centre for Contemporary Studies (NCCS), Kathmandu, Nepal. He served as Professor and Chairman of Political Science Department at Tribhuvan University. He has contributed articles and chapters in different international, national journals and authored & edited books on Nepal and South Asia. He is also the editor of Journal of Contemporary Studies published by the NCCS. He was a member of the delegation to the United Nations General Assembly in 1990, International Research Committee member of Regional Centre for Strategic Studies (RCSS, Colombo), and Nepal's Ambassador to India in 1996-97.

Ambassador Madhu Raman Acharya is currently the Executive Director of the South Asia Centre for Policy Studies (SACEPS). Amb Acharya was Director at the United Nations Assistance Mission to Iraq (UNAMI) and the Permanent Representative of Nepal to the United Nations. During that capacity, he was elected Chairman of the Fourth Committee (Special Political and Decolonization) for the sixty-first session of the General Assembly (2006-07) and he also represented Nepal as the chair of the Global Bureau of the Least Developed Countries (LDCs).He was the Foreign Secretary to Government of Nepal (2001-05) and Nepal's Ambassador to Bangladesh (1998-2001).He has authored few books which include *Business of Bureaucracy* and *Nepal: Culture Shift.*

Ambassador (Dr) Shambhu Ram Simkhada is Member, Secretariat of the Special Committee for the Supervision, Integration and Rehabilitation of the Maoist Army Combatants, Government of Nepal. He is also a member of Peace and Conflict Management Committee of the Government of Nepal. In addition, he is Central Executive Member of International Relations Department of the Nepali Congress Party Dr. Simkhada was Permanent Representative of Nepal to the United Nations, the World Trade Organization and Other International Organizations in Geneva and served as Chairman of the United Nations Commission on Human Rights. He was also Ambassador to Switzerland.

Ms Menaka Guruswamy practices law at the Supreme Court of India. Amongst other cases, she has successfully litigated against state-sponsored vigilante groups *Salwa Judum* in Chhattisgarh, argues a large constitutional case that seeks reform of public administration and the bureaucracy in the country. Menaka has advised the United Nations Development Program (UNDP), New York and the United Nations Development Fund for Women (UNIFEM), New York. She has most recently advised the Government of India on private security agencies and licensing of weapons. She also advises the Constitution-Making process in Nepal. Her most recent publications, include, a piece on regulation of India's intelligence agencies '*Regulating the Gentleman's Game* and *Integration of Combatants and New Constitutionalism in Nepal.*

Mr Lalit Bahadur Basnet an Attroney at Law is currently, Advisor to the President of Nepal. He has served as legal advisor to the Speaker, the House of Representatives, Nepal Water Supply Corporation, Nepal Electricity Corporation, and the Radio Nepal. He holds Masters Degrees in Constitutional Law, Public Administration and Political Science from Tribhuvan University, Kathmandu. He has published many articles in several international and national law journals, newspapers and magazines. He has also authored books on Constitution and federalism. He has presented many papers at various fora.

Mr Ratna Sansar Shrestha is a management professional specializing in financial/economic, managerial and legal aspects of the water resource sector inter alia hydropower projects, renewable/clean energy technologies, rural electrification, environmental enterprises, carbon trading. He is also a Fellow of the Institute of Chartered Accountants of Nepal and a legal practitioner accredited by the Nepal Bar Council. He is also a member of board of directors of Nepal Hydro & Electric Co. (and chair of its Audit Committee). He is also a Visiting Faculty at Kathmandu University School of Engineering and was also associated with the School of Management under Kathmandu University. He was a member of Water Supply Tariff Fixation Commission and also worked as a member of board of directors of Nepal Electricity Authority.

Raju Prasad Chapagain is Chairperson of Justice and Rights Institute-Nepal (JuRI-Nepal). He was associated with the UN Office of the High Commissioner for Human Rights in Nepal (OHCHR-Nepal) in different capacities including Legal Advisor and Thematic Advisor (transitional justice and rule of law). In addition, he worked in various capacities including a Public Interest Lawyer at Pro Public (Forum for Protection of Public Interest) litigating a wide range of constitutional and human rights issues in the Supreme Court of Nepal. He co-founded CLaF (Constitutional Lawyers' Forum) and served it as General Secretary. He has authored a significant number of research articles, papers and opinion pieces on constitutional and legal issues for various national and international publications.

Mr. Chiran Jung Thapa regularly writes on security and strategic issues. He did his Masters from the School of International and Public Affairs, Columbia University. He is at present working with The Asia foundation, Kathmandu. Thapa has also worked in the Permanent Missions of Singapore and Nepal to the United Nations in New York. Prior to that, he also worked with the World Bank and International Finance Corporation.

Dr. Hari Bansh Jha is Professor of Economics and Executive Director of the research organization, Centre for Economic and Technical Studies (CETS) at Lalitpur, Kathmandu, Nepal since 1989. He was senior ICCR Fellow at Institute for Defense Studies and Analyses (IDSA) in New Delhi from 2011-2012. He was also Visiting Scholar at The Institute of Asian Studies, German Institute of Global and Area Studies in Hamburg Germany in 2011. Jha has a M.A. in Economics from Banaras Hindu University and Ph.D. from University of Bihar in India. He also worked as Economic Advisor in the Ministry of Foreign Affairs in Nepal in 1989-90. Dr Jha has to his credit 27 published books. He worked on 55 research projects sponsored by different organizations, including the UNDP, UNICEF, UNCTAD, ILO, WHO, World Bank, USAID, the Asian Development Bank, etc. His interests are wide ranging and include: spirituality, climate change and security, border studies, Nepal-India relations, peace and conflict, Nepal's relations with Tibet/China, migration, and more.

CSA Publications

Books

Conflict Resolution and Peace Building

1. Conflict Resolution and Peace Building in Sri Lanka

2. Federalism and Conflict Resolution in Sri Lanka

3. Peace Process in Sri Lanka: Challenges & Opportunities

4. Conflict over Fisheries in the Palk Bay Region

5. Conflict in Sri Lanka: The Road Ahead

6. Peace and Conflict Resolution: Emerging Ideas

7. From Winning the War to Winning Peace: Post War Rebuilding of the Society in Sri Lanka

8. Internal Conflicts in Myanmar: Transnational Consequences

9. Internal Conflicts in Nepal: Transnational Consequences

10. The Naxal Threat: Causes, State Responses and Consequences

11. Conflict in Sri Lanka: Internal and External Consequences

12. Conflicts in North-East: Internal and External Effects

13. Conflict in Jammu and Kashmir: Impact on Polity, Society and Economy

14. Post Conflict Sri Lanka- Rebuilding of the Society

15. Internal Conflicts: Military Perspectives

16. Internal Conflicts: A Four State Analysis

Security Studies

17. US and the Rising Powers: India and China

18. Maritime Security in the Indian Ocean Region: Critical Issues in Debate

19. Public Perceptions of Security in India: Results of a National Survey

20. Essential Components of National Security

21. Economic Growth and National Security

22. Security Dimensions of India and Southeast Asia

23. India & ASEAN: Non-Traditional Security Threats

24. Emerging Challenges to Energy Security in the Asia Pacific

25. Security Dimensions of Peninsular India

26. Socio-Economic Security of Peninsular India

Civil Society and Governance

27. Civil Society and Governance in Modern India

28. Civil Society in Conflict Situations

29. Civil Society and Human Security: South & Southeast Asian Experiences

Bulletins

1. Nuclear Terrorism and Counter Proliferation: Issues and Concerns; After the Afghanistan and Iraq Wars: Perspectives from the US; Indo-Pak Relation: Limited War to Limited Peace?

2. Unconventional Weapons and Threats of Accidents and Terrorism; The Stability- Instability Paradox: South Asia and the Nuclear Future; Post 9/11: New Research Agenda?; The US and India: Divergent and Convergent Interests

3. Conflict Prevention and Peace Building

4. Indo-Japan Relations; Independent Police Complaints Commission; Brief on the Seminar on Security Dimensions of Peninsular India

5. Proceedings of the Seminar on Proliferation Security Initiative

6. Proceedings of the Seminar on Women and Legal Security

7. Political Islam: Image and Reality; UK and India on the World Stage

8. Proceedings of the Seminar on Women and Comprehensive Security

9. Global Nuclear Weapon Prospects; India-Pakistan Peace Process Dividends

10. Security Perspectives from Pakistan; Indo-US Relations: Changing Perceptions

11. Sri Lankan Peace Process: Current Status; Sri Lanka Today: Policy Challenges and Dilemmas

12. Religion, Civil Society & Governance

13. Politics of the Nuclear Deal and the US-India Relations

14. India –US Relations; Japan India Partnership in the New Asian Strategic Dynamism

15. Environmental Security; National and International Security in the Context of Globalization and Economic Prosperity; India, East and Southeast Asia: Security Dimensions

16. India-EU Relations

17. India-Japan Strategic Partnership; India-UK Economic and Business Partnership.

18. Right to Information

19. A Sustainable Future: India and Britain Working Together; India and Africa: Issues of Globalization and Development

20. New Initiatives in Nuclear Disarmament; Preventing Nuclear Proliferation and Nuclear Terrorism; Nuclear Fuel Supply Assurances

21. The Economic Cost of the War in Sri Lanka; Peace Process in Sri Lanka; The Sri Lankan Diaspora: The Way Forward

22. Nuclear Deterrence and Disarmament

23. Naxalism: Threat to Internal Security; Ethno-Political Situation in India's Northeast.

24. Japan and Asian Security; India as a Superpower.

25. India's Water Relations with her Neighbours

www.ingramcontent.com/pod-product-compliance
Lightning Source LLC
Chambersburg PA
CBHW030333270326
41926CB00010B/1608